Great Train Crimes

Great Train Crimes

Murder and Robbery on the Railways

Jonathan Oates

First published in Great Britain in 2010 by
Wharncliffe Books
an imprint of
Pen and Sword Books Limited,
47 Church Street, Barnsley,
South Yorkshire S70 2AS

Copyright © Jonathan Oates, 2010

ISBN: 978 1 84563 112 3

Printed and bound in Great Britain by CPI UK

Pen & Sword Books Ltd incorporates the imprints of
Pen & Sword Aviation, Pen & Sword Maritime,
Pen & Sword Military, Wharncliffe Local History, Pen & Sword Select,
Pen & Sword Military Classics, Leo Cooper, Remember When,
Seaforth Publishing and Frontline Publishing

For a complete list of Pen & Sword titles please contact:
PEN & SWORD BOOKS LIMITED
47 Church Street, Barnsley, South Yorkshire, S70 2AS, England.
E-mail: enquiries@pen-and-sword.co.uk
Website: www.pen-and-sword.co.uk

Acknowledgements

Many thanks to all who have helped with this book; including, as ever, John Coulter and Reg Eden, and also Jonathan Feldman and Diann McDonald of Broadmoor Hospital. My thanks go out to those who helped more anonymously, including the staff at the National Archives and the British Library Newspaper Library in particular.

This book is dedicated to David, himself a railwayman and the son of a railwayman.

Contents

List of Plates

Introduction

Mention railway crime and many people will think of the Great Train Robbery of 1963. Or perhaps the famous Agatha Christie story, *Murder on the Orient Express*. But there are many more real-life crimes which occurred on trains or at railway stations. Some of these are reasonably well known to crime buffs, such as the first railway murder ever to occur in Britain which was on a North London train in 1864. Most, however, are very obscure and have never been written about since they were committed.

This book aims to survey serious crimes – including murders and significant thefts – which have occurred on Britain's railways and on the London Underground. It does not include the cases where bodies or parts of bodies have been found at railway stations, but where the murders occurred elsewhere. Three such cases occurred in the 1930s, at Waterloo and at Brighton. Nor are the crimes of John Duffy, the Railway Rapist, who also killed three women in 1985–6 on London's suburban rail network, written about here, because these took place near railway stations, not on them or on trains. Most of the crimes chronicled here are given a complete chapter. These include the first ever large-scale robbery on board a train, in which the thieves believed they had escaped scot free, a high-profile assault on a young woman by an army officer, terrorist bombs on the Underground in the 1880s and numerous murders either on board trains or at railway stations. Some of these killings went unsolved, but the majority were cleared up. Then there is a chapter summarizing accounts of other railway crimes which have either have been written about recently or are fictional or are in very recent memory (from the past three decades).

The sources for this book are primarily ones which were created at the time of these crimes. Police files are a principal source. Metropolitan Police files and Assize papers, located at the National Archives, are very useful. They include witness statements, police reports, medical details and other relevant information. Some of this has never been used before. But police files do not always exist; nor are they always open for public inspection. Newspapers, both national and local, have been used. For the Victorian and Edwardian period, newspaper reporting of murders was very detailed indeed. Unfortunately, the column space devoted to them and indeed other news stories declined with time, even though the newspapers increased in page length.

The author has written six books about real-life crime already, but he has only one distant connection with railway crime. His paternal grandmother's sister married into the middle-class Wheater family of Harrogate. One of this family was John Wheater, born in 1920, who became a solicitor. He was involved in the Great Train Robbery of 1963 and was sentenced to three years in gaol, though he had not taken any direct part in the theft itself (he had arranged the acquisition of the hideout in Buckinghamshire for the gang). On his release from gaol in 1966, he said that what he really objected to in prison was having to mix with criminals.

1

The Railways and Crime

*I am not a timid man, but I never enter an English railway carriage
without having in my pocket a loaded revolver.*

Much has been written about British trains and railways. This chapter
aims to give the very briefest of summaries about British railway history
and then to discuss railway crime and railway policing.

The Stockton–Darlington Railway, which opened in 1825 was
Britain's – and the world's – first railway. However, rudimentary railways
had been in use in industrial districts since the sixteenth century, where
coal was transported on carts which ran on rails. What made the
Stockton–Darlington line different was that the train was powered by
steam and that it carried passengers as well as goods. The Manchester to
Liverpool railway of 1830, though, was the first to be powered solely by
steam and carried mainly passengers. Railways were much faster than
other methods of inland transport, such horse power and canals, though
all three methods of transport coexisted for much of the nineteenth
century.

In the 1840s there was an explosion of railway building all over
Britain, known as railway mania, as it was believed the railways were a
way to a quick profit. A leading figure in this was George Hudson of
York, who was not above sharp practice. This was all the work of private
enterprise, the state not seeing for itself any role in administration nor
supervision of them, though permission had to be sought by private Act
of Parliament prior to construction. Many of these railway lines
emanated from London. The first long-distance line was the London
(Euston) to Birmingham railway, inaugurated in 1837. Another was the
Great Western Railway, from London Paddington to (eventually) Bristol,
in the following year. By the later nineteenth century, England was
covered in a network of railways. Many of these train companies

operated small lines and were often short-lived, being soon amalgamated with others.

The coming of the railways was not without criticism. There were many misgivings. Some included the fact that they might disrupt hunting, or that they would pose a health risk to travellers. Conservatives feared that revolutionaries could travel about more easily and quicker. Others thought that criminals from the cities could swiftly travel to the countryside.

Trains had more positive effects, too. They allowed goods to be transported more cheaply. They enabled people to travel around the country more quickly and this led to the breakdown of rural isolation. People saw more of their fellow Britons. Some historians have commented that train travel helped socially unify the island in a way that no other method had done hitherto. They also helped towns and cities to grow, by allowing suburbs to develop, enabling people to live at some distance from their workplace. This was especially the case around London.

In London, the Underground system began in 1863, with the Metropolitan line from Baker Street to Farringdon. Commuter lines were constructed over the following decades, with the District line in the 1880s and the Central line in the early decades of the twentieth century. Electric power replaced steam power in the 1900s. In the 1920s, the different underground companies were amalgamated and nationalized under the London Transport Passengers' Board.

In the later twentieth century, however, the railways underwent a decline. In part, this was because of the increased competition from newer forms of transport, such as buses and cars. The latter became more prevalent as the century progressed. In 1923 there was a huge amalgamation of the hundreds of railway companies which had existed since the previous century into just four large concerns (London Midland and Scotland, Great Western, Southern and London and North Eastern). The Second World War wreaked havoc with the networks and in 1948 they were nationalized, becoming known as British Rail. At this time, there were about 19,000 miles of railway track, 5,000 stations and 1,000 tunnels, much of which would have been familiar to their Victorian forebears. Yet more swingeing change was to come. In the next two decades, thousands of lines of track were taken out of service, mostly after the Beeching Axe of 1963, which closed down many small stations. This led to a loss of identity and economic disruption in the affected areas, but also to the end of trains only carrying six people in a day. Diesel trains replaced steam wholly by the later 1960s. In the 1990s, the railways were controversially returned to private hands.

Without wanting to sound like a spokesman for the railway companies, it is very, very unlikely that railway passengers will be murdered. Since the nineteenth century there have been less than 30 victims, excepting the underground bombings of 2005. Passengers are more likely to die from accidents, such as that at Harrow in 1952 (112 deaths) or that at Southall in 1997 (6 deaths). The worst single Underground accident was in 1975 when 42 people were killed when the train crashed into the barrier at Moorgate. Yet these figures pale in comparison to the thousands killed each year on Britain's roads. As a previous writer on crime on railways has noted:

> statistics indicate that a person boarding a train which is not a football special is more likely to reach his destination unmurdered, not even molested, than if he had chosen some form of transport other than a bullet proof, bomb resistant, self catering, oxygen carrying automobile fitted with a carbon monoxide measuring gauge and driven by a nun.

Another writer, one John Pendleton, in 1894, agreed, 'on English railways the crime of murder has been rare' pointing out that there had, to date, been 28 murders on French railways and only 4 on English trains (though there had been none in Germany).

That having been said, train travellers are not immune from crime any more than travellers in any other form of transport are. Those on ships have risked pirates, and road travellers were once in danger from footpads and highwaymen. However, although the exploits of pirates and highwaymen have been glamorised and sanitised, those of train-board criminals have not, on the whole, been afforded such romanticizing. Perhaps this is because their crimes are all too recent and all too real and still currently dangerous, whereas the likes of the fictional Captain Jack Sparrow and the real life Dick Turpin are safely in the distant past, as far as Britons are concerned.

The first Underground bombings, 1883–1885

I heard an explosion something like the report of a cannon.

It is unlikely that any readers of this book will have forgotten the terrible terrorist bombings on the London Underground on 7 July 2005, when three young Muslim men caused death and injury to hundreds of people. However, few if any among the media pointed out that this was not the first time that bombs had been used on the London Underground. The IRA rarely targeted the Underground, but in the late nineteenth century bombers chose this location for their attack.

Until 1921, Ireland was ruled by Britain. This was resented by many Irish people. Violent attempts had been made to achieve independence in the late eighteenth century and at several times in the next century. In the years 1880–7 this took the form of a dynamite campaign in England and Scotland, with attacks being carried out in Liverpool, Glasgow, Birmingham and London. Some targeted prominent buildings, such as the Tower of London and the House of Parliament. Others were aimed at the railway network.

The first bombs to go off in the Underground tunnels were heard on Tuesday 30 October 1883. One went off about 600 yards from Praed Street (since 1948 incorporated as part of Paddington) station on the Metropolitan line at 7.51 pm as the train was heading towards Edgware, and the other between Westminster station and Charing Cross on the District line, just after 8 pm. In the former instance, there was a flash of white light, followed by a loud explosion. Those on the train were thrown off their feet and injured by glass. The second carriage to the last one suffered the most damage. Although the framework of the carriages was not badly damaged, the windows, door frames and outside panels were shattered. Nearby houses were said to have been shaken.

One witness, Corporal Warren, said:

> All I remember of the explosion was a very bright flash immediately followed by a terrible report like that of a cannon. It was on the outside of the carriage. I was struck by something which knocked me insensible, and when the train arrived at the station I staggered across the platform. I remember nothing more, except that a soldier picked me up.

William George, a fellow passenger, recalled:

> On Tuesday evening I was a passenger from Queen's Road, Bayswater, to Gower Street [known as Euston Square since 1909].

The train was rather full. I was in the last carriage of the train. We passed along alright as far as Praed Street. Afterwards I heard an explosion something like the report of a cannon. I saw a flash, and the lights in our carriage went out suddenly. For one moment I thought it was caused by the lamp in our carriage, but the next moment I found myself scrambling among the other passengers. When I had collected myself I removed from my head a piece of glass about an inch and a half in length. I heard two reports – one a very sharp sound and the other a dull sound. I remembered no more.

The second explosion occurred just as the Mansion House train was pulling into Charing Cross. This was less dangerous, with only lights and windows at the station being blown out. Volumes of black dust from the tunnel enveloped the platform, and at first a gas explosion was suspected. Telegraph lines were cut and trains had to be suspended pending investigations. Windows from the nearby St Stephen's Club were also broken. Fortunately there were no trains in that part of the underground at that time. Mr Killingsworth Hedges, an engineer, remarked, 'That the disaster was in no way due to anything connected with the trains is evident from the fact that at the time it occurred, there was no train in the section between Charing Cross and Westminster.'

About 40 people on the train near Praed Street were injured by these bombs. Most were sent to St Mary's Hospital so that their injuries could be seen to. Dr Owens, the medical superintendent there, oversaw their care. Fortunately, none had life-threatening wounds. Most only suffered cuts from flying glass. Only four people had to be admitted as in-patients. Richard Brown, aged 45, was the most badly hurt. An artery had been cut and he had, at first, bled profusely. Walter Warren, a corporal in the Dragoon Guards, suffered from concussion as well as numerous cuts. Some suffered from shock and others from temporary deafness. Two days after the explosion, all were recovering. Two schoolboys were sent to a nearby hotel for the night and went home the next day.

On 2 November, both the Home Office and the Metropolitan and District Railway companies offered £500 each for the apprehension of the perpetrators. Meanwhile, Colonel Mejendie, an explosives expert employed by the Home Office, had been busily investigating the rolling stock which passed over the lines just before the explosions, as well as interviewing the railway staff who had witnessed the explosions.

Chemistry experts were also employed. Inspector Frederick Abberline, a key officer in the hunt for Jack the Ripper in 1888, was also one of the leading detectives in this case. They found four rockets, but upon examination these turned out to be fireworks of the type used by schoolboys in the run-up to 5 November, not dynamite cartridges. Yet dynamite had been used to cause these explosions.

It was thought that the explosive near Charing Cross was the work of someone on an earlier train. A vessel containing the explosive, and set with a time fuse, was lowered by a piece of string and dropped over the window of the last carriage. It was thought that the string had been measured so the explosive could be slung just above ground level and then could be dropped without causing a premature explosion. Then the string was cut and the time fuse began to burn.

However, that at Praed Street was laid in a hole in the tunnel's brickwork. Apparently there was a ten-minute interval between trains in the case of the latter and men had been allowed to wander into these tunnels. This practice was now cancelled.

Then there was the question as to culpability. Some initially thought that the explosions might have been accidental or the work of discharged railway workers. Yet this was deemed a deliberate plot, similar to that against the local government offices in Charles Street, Westminster, earlier that year. It was thought that the criminals were not men knowledgeable of London, because neither blast damaged any public buildings as that in March had. The aim of the explosions was evidently to cause alarm, wreck trains and injure passengers. However, no one was ever apprehended for either crime.

Yet Londoners did not panic and remained calm. As *The Times* observed on 1 November, 'It is greatly to the credit of the people of London that there has been no approach to panic, still less to any rash impulses of suspicion and vengeance.' Perhaps this was partly because there was no loss of life – when Fenians had killed over a dozen people in Clerkenwell in 1867 with a bomb, some Irish workers in the capital were sacked because of doubtless unjust suspicion against them on account of their nationality. Ironically, it was noted, in 1883, 'If among the dynamite party there was a man willing really to take his life in his hand, the doctrine of spoliation and disruption might have been terribly asserted.' In other words, had this been a case of what would now be termed a suicide bomber, death and devastation would have been high – as was discovered in 2005.

The bombers struck again in February 1884, and this time their plans were more ambitious. There were attempts made to destroy parts of four major London railway stations: Victoria, Charing Cross, Ludgate Hill and Paddington. The only one which actually detonated was at 1 am on Tuesday 25 February at Victoria. It was fortunate that the station was almost deserted and that no lives were lost – a quarter or half an hour earlier and that would almost certainly not have been the case. A large portion of the long frontage of the station was blown to smithereens. Various offices there were completely wrecked and the gas pipes were leaking. Fire broke out, but the station staff contained the blaze until the Fire Brigade could arrive and douse the flames. Apparently at 8 on the previous evening, a respectably dressed man had deposited a portmanteau at the cloakroom, as the attendant recalled. One of the cases was heavy and the gentleman asked it be handled with care. It was this case which was later to be found – or rather the remains of it – at the centre of the area affected by the explosion. Luckily, the clock fuse, which was probably set to 12, went off an hour late.

After the explosion at Victoria, extra vigilance was clearly visible in other major railway termini in London. At Charing Cross, on Wednesday, 27 February, just before midnight, bearing in mind what had happened at Victoria, the cloakroom porter was told to investigate any items which looked suspicious and had been deposited in the cloakroom there. He found a black portmanteau which seemed unusually heavy, and was later found to weigh 27 pounds. It was opened, and beneath some old clothes, and some daily English newspapers of 20 and 21 February 1884, were found cakes of a peculiar nature, which were labelled Atlas Powder. This was an explosive made of pure nitroglycerine and sawdust, added together so it would not explode in handling by its operators, and was manufactured in America. It was illegal to import it into England. There was a detonator attached which should have caused the device to explode, but it had failed to do so. The man who left it may have been about five feet ten, because that was the size of the trousers found within the case.

A similar discovery was made on the afternoon of the same day at Paddington. Two days previously, a brown leather portmanteau, studded with brass knobs of American make, and of a similar weight, had been deposited in the cloakroom there. It was opened and inside were found 46 cakes of Atlas powder, some in a cash box and the others surrounding it. There was a clockwork timer attached, but for some reason, perhaps a faulty mechanism, it had failed to detonate. It was timed to explode at midnight, but the clock had stopped at 9.10. It was exactly the same as the devices found elsewhere. However, in this case there was a copy of the *New York Sun* of 6 February 1884. Although the attendant was questioned about the man who left it, he could give no clue to his identity because on that evening, it had been very busy and usually between 300 and 400 cases were deposited daily. Yet the man depositing the bag was probably reasonably well to do because the case was not inexpensive, costing between 20s and 25s.

It was thought that the men behind the bombing were Americans. This was because the explosive used was American and because of the American newspaper found in one of the portmanteaus. In any case, there was Fenian support in that country. It was also thought that the men who deposited the cases were very conscious of their own safety and took care to be at a distance when the bombs exploded. The dynamite had been timed to explode when there would be large numbers of people at the railway stations.

Two Americans were seen behaving oddly in Windsor on the Friday and Saturday after the bombs had been located. On early Friday afternoon, an American arrived at the town and looked around the castle. He refused the services of a guide. The police were alerted, but after visiting other parts of the town, he disappeared. On the following day, a respectably dressed American went to a pub near the castle and ordered a meal. The landlady thought he was acting oddly, so sent a man to investigate. He found that the American had removed most of his clothing for an unknown reason. The doubtless embarrassed stranger quickly paid up and left. There was also a rumour that an Irishman had been at Charing Cross on Monday and declared that he expected there would be a 'blow-up' there soon, but this was discounted.

Once again, no one was ever convicted of these bombings, despite a combined reward by the government and the railway companies totalling £2,000. It was believed that there were four men involved in all, one to deposit dynamite at each of the four stations. They had arrived, separately, in London on 20 February. One was a man of some social status, aged 28, who had arrived at the Waverley Hotel, Portland Road, at 7 pm, half an hour after the Liverpool Express had terminated its journey at Euston. He had with him an American portmanteau of the same type as those later found at the railway stations. He was about five feet six in height, thin faced and with dark hair and a moustache. Another man, with a similar bag, came to the hotel an hour later. He was about 40, an American, and of medium height with a fair moustache. He carried a similar case. On 25 February, the night when the four explosions were to have occurred, the two men left the hotel, never to return. One of the portmanteaus which had dynamite in it was later shown to hotel staff, who identified it as being similar at least to the luggage carried by the guests just mentioned. If one of the men left his case at Paddington at, it was believed, 5.30 pm, he could then have caught the 5.45 to Weymouth and then boarded a ferry to Cherbourg and so been safely out of the country when the case exploded.

Their two co-conspirators arrived at Waterloo from Southampton at 7.04 pm on 25 February. They had come from America. They took a cab from Waterloo, but the police were unable to trace the cabman who took them to their unknown destination. One man was aged about 29, five feet ten, with a round face, light brown hair and a slight moustache. His companion was perhaps a year older, shorter and bearded. They had a large brown trunk with them. What is odd is how they could have smuggled the explosives, weighing about 100 pounds, through Customs.

All this was undoubtedly part of a Fenian plot. It was thought that the more respectable and peaceful Irish politicians could exert an influence over their more violent colleagues. According to *The Times*:

> They would do well to exert that influence for the repression of outrages, since the British people, however long suffering, will not indefinitely put up with the murder of innocent persons, and may supplement the imperfections of legal machinery with reprisals of an exceedingly unpleasant kind upon the Irishmen whose presence they now tolerate.

Yet there was more to come. As in 2005, the initial explosion on the Friday evening of 2 January 1885 took everyone by surprise. It was 9.15 and it happened in the tunnel of the Metropolitan Line between Gower Street and King's Cross stations. The 8.53 Hammersmith down train from Aldgate was stopped at the Charlton Street box at 9.13. The train had six carriages, most of which was third class. The line was clear and so the signalman allowed the train to proceed at 9.14. Scarcely had the train reached 70 yards from the signal box, travelling at 14 mph, when 'an explosion, attended with a loud report, took place'.

There was a flash. Gas from the train and the signal box were extinguished. All the glass in the train was shattered, as it was in the signal box. The clock in the latter was also smashed and the hands remained set at 9.14. The carriages rocked and people were hurled together on the train, greatly alarming other passengers, as might be imagined. Fortunately, there were few people travelling that evening. It was only when the train stopped at Gower Street that the damage was known.

One witness stated:

> So loud was the report and so strong the concussion that several persons crossing the Euston Road in close proximity to the gratings were thrown off their feet while the horses of the omnibuses and other vehicles were restrained only with great difficulty from running away. At Gower Street station and King's Cross nearly all the lights were put out, and the gas engineer was thrown off his seat on his face. Several women on the platform fainted.

Fortunately, the explosion was not deadly. True, a few people had been hurt by flying broken glass, but that was all. No one died. Mr Macintosh, a gas engineer at Gower Street, saw the train arriving with its lamps out. The train was emptied of passengers and sent to Bishop's Road, Neasden Junction. The carriages had suffered no damage to the woodwork or structure.

Superintendent Harris of S division and Chief Inspector Gosden of the Metropolitan Railway Police arrived on the scene about half an hour later in order to ensure the safety of the public. They examined the tunnel where the explosion occurred. Part of the brickwork there had been blown away (with a diameter of about two feet). There was also evidence that the roof had been affected by the explosion, with the crust of dirt there being blown away. Yet the main structure of the tunnel was sound. The signal box at St Pancras was damaged. The explosion took place on the north side of the line between St Pancras church and the Charlton street signal box.

The debris in the tunnel was also raked through for any clues. But the items found – small scraps of paper, pieces of wood and a boy's cap – did not help the investigation.

The explosion might have been caused by someone throwing a bomb from the passing train from Hammersmith. The bomb could have been dynamite or gun cotton. It might have been a small percussion bomb, of the type used to kill Tsar Alexander II in 1881, which would explode immediately on hitting a hard surface. Nitroglycerine might have been used. It probably fell on the footboard, then rebounded from the tunnel wall and then exploded on impact. One theory was that the perpetrator was the man who was seen to enter a carriage with a parcel and then left at the next station. He was wearing a coat trimmed with fur and wearing a wideawake hat. However, police did not take the latter report seriously.

Further investigations took place on the following day. Colonels Ford and Majendie, inspectors from the Home Office, together with railway officials, went to where the explosion took place. Measures were taken to guard underground tunnels. An appeal was made to all passengers on the damaged train to contact the police with their names and addresses. This was rather tardy, as it could have been done on the night in question, but perhaps the police had not arrived as fast as they should.

Train staff – engine driver, stoker, guard, underguard and signalman – were questioned at the Home Office. None had any previous suspicion of any danger and none had seen any lights beforehand; although some had been on the lookout for any possible danger, given previous explosions. They recalled the explosion was very loud, sudden and like nothing they had ever heard before. The driver recalled there was a puff of smoke as the explosion occurred. None had seen anyone suspicious in the tunnel. But, in any case, since the tunnel was dark it would be unlikely that anyone there would be seen. They had seen no one dash away from the train on reaching Gower Street; indeed the people leaving the train seemed to linger there. Again, the perpetrator would be hardly likely to advertise themselves by running away at first opportunity. In all, the men could shed very little light on the incident.

A critic of both the perpetrator of the crime and the authorities wrote to *The Times*. Although he thought that the explosion 'gives fresh proof to the dynamiters of their own feebleness', the majority of his letter was directed against the police. Vigorous action was needed, as was common sense. Although he gave the police a report about the bombing which he witnessed, he claimed they paid no attention to it. Therefore, he concluded:

> So long as the pursuit of criminals is carried on in this fashion, I can but feel convinced that neither the offer of a reward, however large, nor the extension to England of the Crimes Prevention Act

will be of practical avail in aiding the apprehension of these cowardly scoundrels.

At first it was believed that Anarchists might be responsible for this bomb-throwing outrage. However, it is more likely that it was the work of the Fenians, like the other bombings over the previous two years. There was also a string of unreliable rumours from abroad. The *Gil Blas*, a French newspaper, suggested that the criminals were Irishmen living in Paris. Two were brothers in their thirties. They lived in Montmartre and had been employed in a printing office in Rochechourart until early December 1884, but made the bombs in a cellar and then came to London several weeks before the explosions. Another French newspaper claimed that the criminals were from Les Invalides; another that they were the work of a police plot (recalling the corruption scandal among the detective force in London in 1877) in order to keep up a state of alarm or prevent their own discharge.

Yet on Tuesday 3 February 1885, the police arrested a man whom they believed was responsible for these outrages. The man 'under detention pending enquiries' was an Irish American. Joseph Hammond, the guard of the Gower Street train, thought he had seen the suspect, one James Cunningham, a dock labourer, leave at Gower Street. He remembered him because he had sat in the last compartment but one of the train from Hammersmith, where the brake apparatus was, and this was usually kept empty except in the case of overcrowding, but often did contain passengers' luggage. Of course to travel in this compartment was hardly suspicious in itself, but as a result of the explosion the guard (a former detective constable) kept an eye on the man, who, however, vanished the instant the guard's attention was elsewhere. Hammond gave the police a description of the man and this matched that of Cunningham.

At Bow Street magistrates' court, Cunningham, alias Dalton, and one Harry Burton, a cabinet maker, were charged with high treason and were accused of causing the explosion at the Tower of London on 24 January 1885. Much of this need not concern us, but they were also implicated in the Gower Street bombing. The two had arrived from America, as the 1884 bombers probably had too. Cunningham had been back and forth between America and England in 1884, sailing from New York on 10 December 1884 and arriving in Liverpool ten days later. By 24 December, at the latest, he was in London, having been seen at Broad Street station. He resided at Great Prescot Street, Whitechapel, near to the Tower of London. Burton arrived shortly afterwards and lived in Mitre Square (where, in 1888, one of the Ripper victims was killed), not far away. They had also been seen with brown American luggage cases.

There were a number of witnesses, other than the guard already alluded to, who had seen Cunningham on 2 January. One was Michael Myers, an auctioneer from Clapham. That day he had been to the City for business, travelling by the Metropolitan line. He had returned that evening on the same line from Farringdon. When a westbound Metropolitan train arrived, he made to enter the brake compartment as he had a case of delicate china. There he saw three men, one of whom was Cunningham. At this point in the hearing, Cunningham shouted at him. 'Liar!'

Myers carried on with his recollections. He had wanted to board that part of the train (although he had a second class ticket and this part of the train was third class, luggage was not allowed in the second class part of the train) and Cunningham blocked his entry, declaring, 'You can't come in here'. When Myers asked why not, he was told, 'Because you can't'. Myers was undeterred and remonstrated, 'There are only three of you inside'. Cunningham merely reiterated his previous retort, 'You can't come in'. Myers boarded another carriage and when the train reached Gower Street, after the explosion, he alighted. He noticed that Cunningham and his two companions did likewise. They went to the back of the train and crossed the line. Myers followed them but was prevented from doing so and so lost track of them. On 4 February, he made a statement to the police and five days later he went to the same magistrates' court as he was now in, and when he saw Cunningham in a corridor, he instantly recognized him.

Hammond gave his evidence as mentioned above and then John Seward, a Hyde Park constable and a former army sergeant, who had been on board the train that night. He remembered seeing Cunningham leaning out of a window just as the explosion took place. He had earlier been able to identify Cunningham. Henry Taylor, a railway porter, recalled Cunningham being in the brake car, at least since Bishopsgate. Again, he had previously picked out Cunningham from a group of other men. He thought he looked like an American by his colour and complexion. Police Sergeant Crawford also recognized him. Other evidence concerned the bombing at the Tower.

It was thought that there was enough evidence to send Cunningham to the Old Bailey and it was here that he was tried on 13–18 May 1885. He was found guilty and sentenced to life imprisonment with hard labour and trembled when sentence was given. He was only 22 – a susceptible age when the wrongs of one's fellows are deeply felt – and a not dissimilar age to some of the suicide bombers of 2005.

Policing the railways

Crime occurs on trains because they bring people together for a certain length of time. Many of these people are unknown to one another. A man intent on theft or assault may enter a train and choose an isolated fellow passenger as a victim. In most of the period covered by this book, both were easy because trains did not have corridors nor were open plan. Instead, people entered one of the compartments which made up each carriage. They could then only alight through the door in which they had entered. This meant at a station at which the train stopped. True, doors were not automatically locked as they have been since the 1980s, but getting out between stations was very dangerous. Once in such a compartment, if a passenger was alone, they could then be at the mercy of anyone else who entered. Sometimes, two people might board a train who were known to each other, one of them having criminal intent, knowing that he now had his victim in a position in which he could deal with them without any outside interference. Finally the noise of the train could easily stifle screams or cries for help.

An American writing in the *Derby Mercury* in 1853 – before anyone had been murdered on a British train – wrote thus:

> I am not a timid man, but I never enter an English railway carriage without having in my pocket a loaded revolver. How I am to know that my travelling companion may be a madman escaped from confinement, or a runaway criminal? And what protection have I against their assault, if it should please them?

Much crime which occurs on trains and on the railways is, on an individual basis, petty. Cumulatively it is not so. Ticket dodging is common, as is trespassing, stone throwing, obstacles on the line and vandalism. In 1959, there were 5,500 prosecutions for larceny and 36,160 offences of all types. In the year 2007–8 there were 13,623 cases of trespass and vandalism. In 2008, railway crime cost £260m and added 22p to the cost of each journey. Violent crime is also not uncommon, with 8,727 cases in 2003–4 and in these years there had been a rise in attacks on underground railway staff by 29 per cent on the previous year. Ticket dodging is not new. In 1902, a man went from Stafford to Willesden Junction, travelling first class. When asked for his ticket, he declared that he was an employee and so did not need one. This was found to be untrue and he was fined 40s (the fare was 20s 9d). As the magistrate said, 'You travel like a king without paying a farthing'. Then there was also theft – £3,500 of gold was stolen from GWR trains in 1848–9 – and rarest of all, murder. David Stephenson in 1853, wrote, 'Thieves are pilfering the goods from our wagons here to an impudent extent.'

What could deal with this menace, other than the common sense of the passengers and train staff? There were a plethora of police forces, whose jurisdictions overlapped. Most well known were the Metropolitan Police, founded in 1829 and who covered Middlesex and London from 1839. They would investigate serious crime committed on any trains in their jurisdiction. Outside London there were the county and borough police forces, of which there were very many until amalgamations in the twentieth century.

Perhaps most importantly of all, there were police forces employed by the railway companies themselves to combat crime occurring on their trains. It is possible that the first railway police predate the Metropolitan Police. There is reference to superintendents and constables as early as 1825 for the Stockton–Darlington Railway, but these men may only have been employed to check tickets, not to deter criminals. Certainly in the 1840s, GWR policemen had to give and receive signals on the line, direct people in and out of stations, protect company property, assist in case of accidents and prevent obstructions on the line. But as the century progressed, they created forces which did specifically combat crime, although some were quicker off the mark than others – the London, Brighton and South Coast line did not have a police force until 1900. Other early railway police forces included the London and Birmingham Railway one, with, in 1840, a force comprising of a superintendent, 10 inspectors and 90 constables. In 1841, there was one railway policeman for each mile and a half of GWR track. By 1920, the South East and Chatham railway police force numbered 181 officers.

Initially, as with the other police forces in the country, pay was low, hours long and discipline strict. The GWR policeman worked twelve-hour days for £1 per week in 1841. Sergeants received £1 2s and inspectors 25s. Singing on duty was frowned on, drunkenness a sackable offence and attendance at church was also expected. However, as with working conditions generally, conditions improved throughout the century and a small annual leave entitlement was granted. By 1902 an eight-hour day was the norm, but a man had to work six days a week. They led the way in some innovations, such as using female officers and also dogs in police work, in the 1900s.

In 1923, with the amalgamation of the railway companies under the Railway Act, four forces were created, each under a chief of police. In 1949, the British Transport Commission was created out of these four forces, which also included canal and dock police. At this time there were 3,700 officers and it was the third largest police force in the country, after the Met and the Lancashire Constabulary. In charge was a chief constable and the country was divided into six geographical areas. Each area was headed by a chief of police and had a CID division. Each area was subdivided into divisions, headed by superintendents, and then into districts, headed by inspectors. With the establishment of a training centre at Tadworth in 1946 and a national headquarters at Park Royal, London in 1959, the force became increasingly professional. The London Transport Police were incorporated in 1958. In 1962 the force was called the British Transport Police. They were made up of uniformed and plain-clothed officers. In the 1980s, the canal and dock forces were separated from the railway police. In 2008, there were 2,835 transport police throughout the UK and 1,455 support officers and they were divided into seven geographical regions.

Some railway policemen were very efficient and dedicated to their duty indeed. In 1845, Sergeant Williams of the GWR was alerted by telegraph that John Tawell, a killer, was on a train from Slough to Paddington. He followed him from Paddington and then apprehended the man. In 1895 a railway policeman, DS Robert Kidd, was killed by thieves when trying to prevent theft from a railway siding in Wigan and a similar incident occurred in Glasgow in 1960, when Walter Macmillan was murdered. On the other hand, the railway police who attempted to investigate the killing of Miss Camp on a suburban train in 1897 managed by their muddling to obliterate any clues there might have been. As Stephenson wrote in 1853, about the railway police, 'wonderful people these detectives. They don't find out everything, though.' We shall now investigate their struggle against assorted villainy.

2

The Gold Bullion Robbery, 1855

'it really is lamentable to reflect upon the amount of skill, dexterity, perseverance and ability exercised upon the execution of a criminal design, which this robbery displays.'

Some readers may have seen the film, *The First Great Train Robbery* (1978) starring Sean Connery (playing William Pierce), Lesley-Anne Down (playing one 'Miriam', Pierce's mistress) and Donald Sutherland (playing Edward Agar). Michael Elphick plays James Burgess. These gentlemen criminals aim to steal gold designated for the Crimean War from a train travelling from London to Dover in 1855. They manage to make copies of the four keys held by the directors of the railway company. Although they are successful, one is arrested, but he makes his escape at the end of the film. So much for the fiction. Now for the facts.

William Pierce (born in 1816), described in 1857 as 'a grocer and imperfectly educated', and Edward Agar (1817–81) had known each other for some years. They appear to have been introduced by James Townsend Saward (born in 1799), a barrister, forger and master criminal. Pierce had worked for the South Eastern Railway Company as a ticket printer until about 1850, when he was dismissed for suspected theft. He had expensive tastes, but little money. Agar had been well educated and once worked legally for a Mr Davis in Chiswell Street; he also made money by speculation. Or so he said; he was notoriously vague on this point and the likelihood was that he was a professional criminal. Forgery seems probable. Pierce and Agar had, in about 1850, discussed the possibility of stealing a large shipment of gold from a railway company whilst it was in one of their trains. Agar later recalled, 'but I had decided, because as I thought, that the thing was impracticable, it could not be done'. Yet there had recently been a robbery from a train near Bristol, in which the thieves had escaped scot free. Agar then spent some time in America.

Agar returned in about 1853. The two met by chance in King Street, Covent Garden, in London, where Pierce was then employed as a clerk in Clipson's betting office. He lived in Walnut Tree Grove, Lambeth. Neither man had forgotten their previous discussion. Pierce recalled:

> I said I believed it was impossible to do it unless an impression of the keys could be procured; and he then said he thought that he could get an impression if I would undertake the business. We had several meetings after that, at all of which the conversation turned upon the subject of getting impressions. He repeated that he thought he could get them; and I said that if he did I had no objection to undertake to complete the robbery.

It is worth stating both the prize which the criminals were in pursuit of and the difficulties which lay in their path. Trains of the South Eastern Railway Company ran from London Bridge to Folkestone and Dover and then to Paris. Sometimes they carried an immense amount of gold bullion. This could amount to over £10,000 – an incredible sum of money indeed. However, the gold was well protected. It was in locked chests and kept in the guard's van, which was locked and, in any case, the public were not allowed admittance there. The chests were regularly checked by being weighed to see that all was as it should be. This was a case where brute force would not suffice. Dynamite had yet to be invented. Cunning, audacity and care would be needed if the criminals were to be successful.

Once Pierce had convinced Agar that he could make copies of the keys to the chests, Agar then asked who else would be involved. Pierce told him that they would be joined by William George Tester (born in 1830) and James Burgess (born in Ipswich in 1821). These men were both employed by the South Eastern Railway Company. Burgess was a guard (since May 1842 he had worked at London Bridge station). Tester was a more recent recruit – he was not working for the company in 1851, but was a station superintendent at Margate station in 1854. Both lived in Lewisham. Tester was a vain dandy and looked to any scheme for making money with enthusiasm. Pierce knew Burgess from his time working for the same railway company. Once the four had become acquainted with each other, the operation could begin. It was to be a well planned and long drawn out affair.

In the autumn of 1853, Agar went to meet Tester at Margate first of all. Agar had tea with him and stayed with him at his lodgings. On the next day, Agar was shown the safe in the station office, and the key to the cash box. Tester asked him if there would be any problem in his copying such a key. 'Not the least', Agar replied. Tester added that it was unfortunate that Pierce had not mentioned such a scheme when he was employed at Folkestone, because then he had custody of the keys in his post of clerk there.

Agar then returned to London. Little of note happened until the following May. Then he and Pierce went to Folkestone to spy out the land. As Agar said, 'the best thing would be to go to Folkestone, to take apartments there, watch the trains in and out, and so discover whether the keys to the bullion chest were there, and how they were to be got at'. They hired an apartment consisting of two bedrooms and a sitting room. It was near to the railway station. Both men went under assumed names; with Agar being known as Adams. They stayed there for two weeks.

Each day they went to the harbour to await the arrival of the train from London and the boat that would take the train's valuables to Boulogne. Agar recalled, 'we carefully watched the iron safe to see whether it was unlocked, and what was done with the keys'. Yet their stay at Folkestone did not run entirely smoothly. Pierce was noticed by the police and Mr Hazel, inspector of the Folkestone police, was on his track. Agar thought that their constant presence in the town without any obvious reason to be there was seen as suspicious and that the police might have thought that Pierce was a pickpocket. Pierce managed to shake the police off his trail and then returned to London, whilst Agar stayed for a few more days before joining him.

Their stay in Folkestone had been very productive indeed. Agar recalled:

> we had noticed generally all the circumstances connected with the arrival and departure of the bullion chest and upon one occasion we had seen it opened. It was placed on the platform, and a man named Sharman came and locked it with one key, which was attached by a loop to a label, from which another key was suspended, which I suspected to be the other key to be required for the safe. I watched Sharman deposit these keys in the cash box.

Agar also noticed that Sharman spent some of his leisure time playing billiards with his colleagues.

The next step was for Agar to be introduced to Thomas Sharman, who had been employed at Folkestone as a booking clerk since May 1849, by one of his colleagues, Tester. The idea was that Sharman could show Agar the crucial keys. In the late summer of 1854, Tester and Agar met in Folkestone 'by accident'. Agar stayed at the Pavilion Hotel. One Sunday he saw Tester and Sharman at the railway station. They walked arm in arm to the harbour station and Agar was introduced to Sharman as planned. The three then went to the Pavilion Hotel for some refreshment.

That evening, Agar and Tester dined together. The latter asked Agar if he thought the robbery could be successful. He replied that, having had an introduction to Sharman, it should be possible. Tester returned to London and Agar spent time with Sharman. However, as Agar admitted, 'he being a very sedate young man', little information could be gained from him. This could have been because Hazel had told him that Agar was 'a suspicious person'. Agar was despondent, reporting back to Burgess and Pierce that he thought the scheme should be put on hold for some time.

Meanwhile, Pierce had received a letter from Tester with news about changes in the security arrangements. One of the keys to the bullion chest was lost and the chest was to be sent to Chubbs so it could be fixed with a new lock. Tester (now employed at London Bridge station) was asked to provide wax impressions of the keys, but Agar objected. He said that he must take the impressions himself. He and Tester met by appointment at the Arcade near London Bridge station. Tester did not have both keys and they had several other meetings, but to no avail. Afraid that they might be seen together there, they decided to meet at a tavern in Tooley Street instead. Tester, in his new position, was eventually able to provide one of the two keys needed and an impression was made by his colleague.

With one key duplicated, Agar returned to Folkestone. He had hitherto sent a box to the railway offices there, which he would collect, under the name of Archer. It was not there on the first day, but he was able to collect it on the Sunday following. He saw how it arrived; being carried in the bullion chest and then taken to the lower station. A Mr Chapman opened the two locks on it. Agar noticed that the keys with which he unlocked it were taken from a cupboard in the office. After he signed for the box, he went back to London.

Once there, he met his confederates again. He told them where the keys were kept. Pierce and Agar went down to Dover and stayed at the Rose Inn, near the church. They then walked over to Folkestone to await the boat from Boulogne. They waited for Chapman and Ledger to leave the railway office. Then they entered; Pierce going to the cupboard for the key and Agar standing guard at the door. Agar took a wax impression of the key and then Pierce returned it to the cupboard. On the same day they returned to Dover and then to London.

Burgess was told the good news and promised Agar, 'It is a good job, and I will do my best to assist you.' There were then a number of meetings between the three of them at The Marquis of Granby pub in New Cross. Agar made keys from the wax impressions, working at Pierce's house in Lambeth. At this time, Agar started living with one Fanny Poland Kay, and their illegitimate newborn child. He had been introduced to her by Burgess in 1853 and she was to play an important part in the outcome of this account, though not in the planning or execution of the theft itself. Pierce moved to Crown Terrace, Hampstead Road, and Agar and his family went to rooms in Cambridge Villas, Shepherd's Bush.

Agar now needed to test whether his keys actually could open the locks on the bullion chest. He arranged with Burgess to travel to Folkestone with him. They went down together at least seven times. At last Agar succeeded, with Burgess looking on as the guard in the train, in opening the bullion chest. Tester could see to it that Burgess would be the guard on the train, and indeed, it was later remarked upon that having him as guard on the same train for two months was highly irregular. But it was a risk that had to be run for not even Tester knew when a consignment of gold would be delivered.

The thieves calculated that two of them could carry a maximum of £12,000 worth of gold bullion. Pierce and Agar went to a shot tower by Hungerford Suspension Bridge. They bought a hundred weight of shot and took it to Agar's rooms. It was there placed in two checked carpet bags. Four courier bags were also made to order in a shop near Drury Lane and some shot placed in these. Agar said that his family did not see any of this activity. The courier bags were made of leather and tested to check that they would carry shot. Agar had them strengthened when he found they were inadequate at first. The carpet bags of shot were taken by cart to Pierce's house. Tester had a black bag ready to take down to Redhill, so he could then carry some of the gold back to London after the theft and relieve his confederates of the burden.

Everything was then ready for the theft to take place. Unwittingly, they rehearsed the final stages several times. Pierce, Burgess and Tester were to meet at London Bridge station, once Burgess was on the train. Finally Agar and Pierce were to take the bags with them and travel by cab to St Thomas Street. Pierce was heavily disguised. Agar alighted and met Tester at the station. Tester told him that there was no gold on board the train.

It was on the sixth such trip that the theft could finally occur. It was 15 May 1855. Pierce and Agar were at a pub in Camden Town. They took a carriage to St Thomas Street. Agar approached the station and saw Burgess at the entrance, wiping his face. This was the signal that they had been waiting for: the bullion was on the train at last.

That night, three boxes containing gold were delivered by their owners to Messrs Chaplin & Co., a transporting firm. These boxes were the property of Messrs Abell & Co., Messrs Spielmann and Messrs Bult. The gold therein was worth in total at least £12,000. At Chaplin's, the boxes were bound with iron hoops, sealed with wafers and were then weighed. On arrival at London Bridge station, they were put into two iron safes. John Chaplin arrived with them and later attested, 'no one at the railway station would know that bullion was being sent over to Boulogne that night until he arrived there with it'. Edgar Cox, the stationmaster's clerk, received the three boxes of bullion from Chaplin. The boxes were chalked up and put outside the stationmaster's office. He weighed them and John Bailey, a porter, put them into the iron safes and Mr Wetherall the stationmaster locked them.

Burgess returned to the station and the other two took the cab to the Dover railway office. En route, Tester was told that everything was alright. Agar then bought two first class return tickets to Dover for himself and Pierce.

Pierce entered a first class compartment alone. As for Agar, as he recalled: 'I walked up and down the platform till the train started, and saw the carpet bags given to Burgess . . . Having watched for my opportunity, I at last jumped unobserved into Burgess' van.' The train left London Bridge station at 8.30 pm. Burgess assigned other duties to John Kennedy, the under guard, so as not to disturb Agar. He crouched down in a corner and was hidden by Burgess. He could soon get to work. There were two iron safes in the van. He opened these and found inside them a number of wooden boxes. He used pliers and wooden wedges to open them. There were four gold bars in the first. Three were put into a carpet bag and one into Tester's bag and given to Burgess. An appropriate amount of shot was put into the box.

By this time the train had pulled into Redhill station at 9.04 pm. Agar heard Tester speak, but did not see him and Burgess gave the bag to Tester. Once the train began moving again, Burgess was in the guard's van with Agar. The latter opened another box and found a quantity of American gold coins there. Other boxes were opened and as much gold was removed as they felt they could carry. About £6,000–£7,000 worth of gold could not be taken as it would have been too heavy. Then the boxes, weighted with lead shot, were all carefully resealed with wax and wafers which Agar had brought with him. They were returned to the safes and locked. Agar then recounted the next step, 'The safes from which I took the gold were removed from the train by the railway company's officers at Folkestone, and we went on with the train to Dover.' It was now 10.30. Richard Hart, porter at Folkestone, took the safes to the harbour, along with Burgess, and delivered them onboard the boat.

Pierce and Agar alighted from the train and took the bags with gold in them with them. They went to the Dover Castle Hotel and had supper. It was now 11 pm. They planned to return to London by the 2 am train. Once they had returned to the railway station, an unexpected nuisance occurred. Agar recalled, 'on a railway porter asking us for our carpet bags, I refused to give them to him, but the man persisted in his request, and almost forced the bags out of my hands'. The two men travelled back to London. Burgess was the guard on this train, too.

Once in London, at 4 am, they called for a cab to take them to Paddington station, but did not ask the porter at the railway station to order one for them. Before they arrived, they told the cab driver that they wished to go to Euston instead. They alighted there and after paying the fare, found another cab to take them to Pierce's house. They then had the problem of converting the gold into cash. Some of it was melted down in a furnace constructed at Agar's house; some of it was sold through intermediaries. One James Saward, a crooked barrister, was one such, and he earned a commission on each ounce of gold he sold. The two later moved to Kilburn. When the four split the initial proceeds; Pierce, Tester and Agar had £600 each and Burgess, £700.

Meanwhile, once the boat arrived at Boulogne, the three boxes were removed from the safes and weighed. Two boxes weighed less than they did in London; the other weighed a little more. The boxes were weighed again in Paris and were found to weigh the same as they had in Boulogne. Monsieur Everard, who was expecting the box sent from Abell's, recalled, 'I saw the box opened. It contained nothing but a quantity of shot and some shavings'. Extensive investigations revealed that the gold could not have been stolen after it left Folkestone. Suspicion was directed towards Burgess as he had been the guard on the train from London to Folkestone. Although he admitted that he sometimes allowed gentlemen to ride in the guard's van, he said he had not done so on the night of the robbery. His length of service and the fact that he answered the questions put to him in a convincing manner were taken as proof of his innocence. A reward of £300 was offered by the railway company. It was not until the end of the year that the South Eastern Railway admitted responsibility: that the theft had taken place aboard one of its trains.

However, although the theft had been a great success from the view of the gang, matters began to unravel in the following months. In August 1855, Agar was arrested and found guilty of forging cheques. In October, he was sentenced to transportation to Australia for life, though he denied he was guilty. At least he could take consolation in the knowledge that Pierce had promised to use his share of the money to keep Fanny Kay and their son in a comfortable lifestyle, by giving her £1 a week. Pierce did so at first, and then in January 1856 decided not to and kept the money all for himself. After arguments, she went to the prison and railway authorities to tell what she knew. The police went to Agar's rooms and found remains of the furnace and gold there.

Agar's former confederates were arrested by the end of 1856; Tester was the last to be caught as he had subsequently taken a post in the Swedish Railways (ironically, his former employers had given him a glowing testimonial for this job) and was only taken when he returned to England to visit his family. Thus Pierce, Burgess and Tester found themselves at the bar of the Old Bailey as prisoners in January 1857. They were charged with robbing the train of its gold. The principal witness for the prosecution was, of course, their former confederate, Agar. However, there were over 30 witnesses who could help verify Agar's story: cab drivers, railway officials, neighbours, buyers of gold, Fanny Kay, as well as various policemen. All three pleaded not guilty.

However, the weight of the evidence was overwhelming. The judge referred to Pierce thus, 'A greater villain than you are, I believe, does not exist'. Pierce was sentenced to two years in gaol with hard labour, and three months of solitary confinement. The others were transported to Australia for fourteen years each. The disparity between sentences was because Burgess and Tester had been working for the South Eastern Railway Company when they had committed the crime and it was a greater offence to betray a confidence than otherwise. But for Pierce's withholding money from Fanny, all would have been well for them. The price of greed was high indeed.

Burgess and Tester were put onboard the ship, *The Edwin Fox*, which arrived in western Australia on 21 October 1858. Burgess was given his ticket of leave on 21 December 1859; Tester on 14 July 1859. This meant that they were on probation. They could work anywhere in the district, but had to report periodically to a magistrate and could not leave the district without permission. Burgess was given a conditional pardon on 21 March 1862; Tester on 17 October 1861. They were freed of the restraints just mentioned, but could not return to England until their term was over. From 1861–3, Tester was clerk of works to a convict establishment and then left Australia on a ship called *The York*. Their ultimate fates are unknown.

Although all the recovered gold was returned to the railway company, about £1,500 belonging to Agar was put in a trust fund for Fanny and her child (who was never named in proceedings). Meanwhile, Agar was sent to Australia on *The Nile*, arriving before his former confederates, on 1 January 1858. On 17 September 1860 he was granted ticket of leave and given a conditional pardon on 13 September 1867. On 30 December 1869, he left for Colombo. Whilst in Australia, he was told, by a newly arrived convict, that his name was a legend in London's criminal fraternity, to which he replied, 'That means nothing, nothing at all.' Agar died in exile in 1881. Saward, incidentally, was sentenced to be transported to Australia for forgery in 1857.

The reader will, if acquainted with the 1978 film, note various differences. Tester is excluded. Miriam, who helps her colleagues in the plot does not resemble Fanny Kay, who played no role in the actual crime or its plotting, nor does the film feature a baby. There are four keys to be taken in the film, not two. Perhaps most importantly, Pierce is arrested near the end of the film, and then triumphantly escapes at its close – a far cry from the initial success and then the squalid climax of reality. The film is really a romanticized version of reality, though as fiction it works splendidly, with acting, scenery, costumes, plot and soundtrack being of the first order.

3

The First Railway Murder, 1864

'An event took place which excited an extraordinary sensation
of surprise and alarm in the public mind and continued
for several months.'

Perhaps it is a tribute to the law-abiding nature of mid-Victorian Britain that it was almost four decades after the first passenger-carrying train that a murder was committed on one of them. Or perhaps it was the conservative and unimaginative nature of the criminal classes.

Thomas Briggs appeared to be the embodiment of the prosperous middle-class, middle-aged Victorian; perhaps a character out of Dickens. He had been born in about 1795 in Cartmel, Lancashire, where he had attended the grammar school. His family were middle-class and Anglican. However, he had lived in London since he was 16, and in Hackney since the late 1830s. In London he began working at Sir John Lubcock's bank. Briggs was hardworking, courteous and of sound judgement. In 1864, he was about 69 and was chief clerk (the highest post below that of partner) at Messrs Robarts & Co. of Lombard Street in the City of London (they had taken over the firm he previously worked for). At death, he was worth between £2,000 and £3,000. Although he had suffered a severe illness and went to Lancashire to recover, by 1864, he was in good health for a man of his age. Briggs was tall and bearded. He lived in a house on Clapton Square, near Hackney parish church. With him lived his wife, Margaret aged 70, and three of his adult children. Of his two sons, one was an insurance clerk and the other a ship broker in the City. They had two domestic servants: a cook and a housemaid. He was highly respected and had many friends. Yet his ultimate fate was a most unfortunate one.

The day began as any other did; like most salaried employees, he led a life of routine. He spent most of Saturday 9 July 1864 at work and at

3 pm left his office. He travelled to see his niece, who lived in Nelson Square, Peckham, arriving at 5 pm. He dined there and at 8.30 left. His niece and her husband, David Buchan, a woollen warehouseman, saw Briggs take an omnibus outside the Lord Nelson pub on the Old Kent Road. This was 15 minutes' walk from their house. Briggs seemed well and was perfectly sober. He had told them of his route home – to the City, then to take a train from Fenchurch Street to Hackney station, arriving at 10 and so home. There were two or three other passengers on the omnibus, besides the conductor and driver, and its eventual destination was Islington. However, Briggs would have alighted at the corner of King William Street, the nearest stop to Fenchurch Street, and the journey should have taken about 20 minutes.

It was about 9.45 when Briggs arrived at Fenchurch Street station. Thomas Fishbourne, ticket collector there, knew Briggs as a regular traveller on the line, and saw him at this point. Briggs was alone and greeted Fishbourne before going up to the platform. Several other people came up after he did. On the platform was William Petrie, who was in charge of the electric telegraph at the station. He and Briggs exchanged greetings. About 15 others joined the train there, but Petrie did not see Briggs board. The train was five minutes late and did not depart until 9.50, stopping at Stepney, then Bow. Briggs entered the first class compartment in the carriage nearest to the engine.

It was at Bow that one Thomas Lee of Parkfield Villas, Hackney, apparently saw Briggs. Lee was standing on the platform and had a few words with his friend. He was surprised to see him out at such a late hour, but more importantly noted that there were two other men in the same compartment:

> I observed two men in the carriage with him. Mr Briggs was sitting with his back to the engine, and appeared in his usual health and spirits. I saw by his side a dark, thin man, apparently tall, and opposite to him I observed a stoutish man, thick set with light whiskers. He had his hand in the loop of the carriage windows, and I noticed that his hand was unusually large.

Lee then went into another compartment (a second class one) and journeyed to Hackney, unaware that Briggs had been assaulted until two days later.

At just after 10 pm, at Hackney Wick, Semple Jones and Harry

Verney, ironically enough clerks at the same bank as Mr Briggs, entered compartment no. 69, a first class compartment. It was covered in blood. Calling a guard, one Haines, they found that the cushions and windows were bloodstained and there was much blood on the floor. But there was no body. The only other evidence that somebody had been there were a hat and a stick, both found under the seat, and a black leather bag. The guard took charge of these and locked the compartment door. He telegraphed Mr Keeble, the stationmaster at Bow, news of this discovery and the two thought that a suicide had occurred, with the unfortunate individual throwing themselves out of the moving train, though this would hardly account for the bloodstained compartment. The train then proceeded to Camden.

Meanwhile, at about 10.15, an equally disturbing discovery was made by the line between Old Ford Bridge and Hackney Wick station. The driver and stoker of the train from Stratford were about to pass the railway bridge over Ducket's canal, by the side of the Milford Arms Tavern and Victoria Park. At first, Alfred Eakins, the driver, thought that it was the body of a dog, but his colleague, John Brinckley, thought otherwise. The train had passed the object before they could stop. Taking a lamp, Brinckley alighted and walked back towards it.

He was right in his original supposition. This was the bloodstained body of a man. Brinckley called out to Eakins, who then went to the nearby pub to ask for assistance. Mr White, the landlord, and some of his customers, came with him and removed the body to the pub. In doing so, they nearly lost their lives by the arrival of a train coming in the opposite direction.

Once the body had been taken to the pub, and laid on a couch, it became clear that he had been the victim of a bloodthirsty assault and robbery. Although the hook of his watch chain was attached to his waistcoat, both chain and watch were not there. His head had been battered by a sharp instrument. White then sent for doctors and the police. Three surgeons arrived – Mr Alfred Brereton of Old Ford was the first to appear (at about 11 pm), followed by Mr Garman of Fairfield Road, Bow, and Mr Vincent Cooper of Coburn Road. He was taken upstairs and then the three examined the injured man, who was not, after all, quite dead, though he was insensible. There were a number of wounds to the head. Stimulants were applied to try and render him conscious, but to no avail.

PC Edward Dougar was on duty at Wick Lane at 10.20. He heard that a man had been found near the line and went to the pub with the others. After calling for a surgeon, he recalled that:

> I searched his pockets to ascertain who he was. His shirt front was rumpled and there was one black stud in it. A bunch of keys, four sovereigns, and some silver were in his left hand breeches pocket and in the other another bunch of keys and 8s 6d in silver and coppers. In his waist coat pocket there was a first class return ticket, and in his coat pocket I found his letters, papers and a silver snuff box. There was a patent fastening attached to his waist coat pocket for a gold chain, and there was a diamond ring upon his finger. There was no watch or chain on him.

Inspector Kerressey of K division arrived from Bow Police Station. He looked at the letters found on the body. They were addressed to Thomas Briggs at his business address on Lombard Street. Kerressey sent a man to check at the bank to confirm Briggs's identity and to find his personal address. This was swiftly accomplished and then the melancholy news had to be broken to the family.

Thomas Briggs, junior, a 28-year-old insurance clerk, and other family members accompanied Mr Francis Toulmin, FRCS, the family doctor, to the tavern. It was now just after 3 am on Sunday morning. Distressing scenes followed, but the injured man could only gurgle in recognizing the voice of an elderly female servant. News of what had happened had leaked and many people gathered outside the pub, such was their interest and excitement. The four doctors remained with Briggs for the remainder of the night and in the following morning, on Toulmin's advice, he was conveyed in a litter to his home. Despite his robust constitution, the old man died at 11.45 pm on Sunday 10 July. This was now no longer robbery with violence, but a case of murder.

Toulmin then undertook a post mortem, in the presence of Brereton and Cooper. There was a jagged wound on the left ear. On the scalp were several severe wounds. The hands and left forearm were grazed and bruised, an indication that the man had tried to defend himself. The skull was also fractured. Some of these injuries would have resulted from the fall from the train. Death was due to the fracture of the skull and the depression of the brain.

Meanwhile, the police investigation proceeded. The younger Briggs was eager to assist with what little information he could. He told them how his father had left for work as normal the day before. He added that he was wearing a gold watch with an Albert chain, and that he wore gold glasses. The watch had been given to his father by a friend about two years before. He also stated that the hat, stick and bag which were found in the compartment were his father's. However, on closer examination, he announced that the hat was not his father's. This hat was to assume great importance in what transpired, because, of course, it must have belonged to the murderer.

Kerressey had details of the missing watch and glasses sent to all police stations in London. He then examined the compartment where Briggs had been attacked. Once the train of which it had been part of reached Camden Town station, the carriage was uncoupled and brought back to Bow where it was put into a shed. It was composed of three first class compartments. There was blood on the brass handles of the door, suggesting the assailant had opened the window in order to throw his victim out. On the floor was found a link from the watch chain and on the footstep was part of the glasses.

The initial police theory was that Briggs had been attacked shortly after the train left Bow. His attacker or attackers wanted to throw him into the canal, but had been unable to do so. One Mr Edward Carr wrote to *The Times* with a theory of his own. This was that Briggs had ruptured one of his arteries and then had jumped from the train in order to procure medical assistance. Others poured scorn on this, pointing out that if this was the case, then whose hat was it that had been found in the compartment and who had closed the carriage door?

The inquest began on 18 July at Hackney Vestry Hall. Mr Toulmin gave the medical evidence and then Mrs Buchan told what she knew. The question of motive was raised. She did not know of anyone who had threatened her uncle. However, her uncle had refused someone a loan and a third party told her that the man who had been turned down had threatened Briggs, though she had assumed that this was not a threat to kill him. Her husband had also heard of this, but not at first hand. Oddly enough, in Briggs's pocket book were two IOUs made out from Buchan. William Townsend, a ticket collector at Hackney Wick, said that it would be easy for anyone to leave the station without passing him at the entrance, because they could exit by the embankment and many of the 'rougher sort' who used the train there often did so.

The doctors reported that, on the following day, they were shown a stone near to the place where Briggs was found. It weighed about half a pound and there was blood and hair attached to it. This stone fitted one of Briggs's head wounds. The inquest was then adjourned until 23 July.

Further information was being found by the police. A lad told them that he had been travelling on the same train as Briggs. He had boarded at Stepney and noticed a tall, dark man walking up the platform, looking in at the occupants of the train. He then entered a compartment where an elderly gentleman sat. It will be recalled that Lee thought that one of the men with Briggs was tall, too. The police were also keeping an eye on the man (unnamed) who had allegedly threatened Briggs.

One of the most important witnesses was Jonathan Matthews, a cab driver, who reported to the police on 18 July. He had known one Francis Muller for two years. He recalled that in December 1863 Muller admired his hat. In exchange for a waistcoat, Matthews bought a similar hat for 10s 6d from Mr Walker's hat shop in Crawford Street, Marylebone. He had seen Muller in this hat in June 1864, and was able to describe the hat before he was shown the one at the scene of the murder. He said:

> I believe this to be the hat that I purchased for him; it corresponds exactly – before I bought it, out of the shop I had it turned up a little at each side – after I had purchased it I said I should like it turned up the same as the one I had the week previous, consequently they did it while I was there – I noticed that there was a little curl in the brim.

When asked why he did not tell the police until over a week after the murder, he said that he had not seen a newspaper since then, though some claimed he was waiting for a reward to be offered. At that time it stood at £300 and Matthews was in debt.

What appeared to be another important new development occurred at 1 pm on 20 July. John Haffa, a German tailor, who lived at Park Terrace, Old Ford Road, Bow, went to the offices of the City of London Police. He told Inspector Hamilton that four days after the assault, he had purchased a pawnbroker's ticket for 12s from Francis Muller. Muller had lodged at the same house as Haffa and the two had known each other for several months. The pawnbroker's ticket was

worth 30s and was for a gold watch chain that had been pledged at Mr
Annis's shop in the Minories on the afternoon of 12 July. Muller and
Haffa had recently worked together for a Mr Hodgkinson on
Threadneedle Street, but Muller had argued with the foreman, lost his
job and decided to start a new life in America, enlisting in the Union
army in the ongoing American Civil War (1861–5). To do so, he needed
some ready money to pay his fare, so sold the ticket at a loss. Muller had
then took a ship to New York, on 14 July, travelling from the London
Docks.

This led the police to the jewellery shop of one John Death in
Cheapside. On the Monday after the murder, Briggs's watch chain had
been exchanged for another at Death's shop. Robert, Death's brother,
who was running the shop on the day in question, recalled:

> On Monday morning, July 11, a young man of about 30, with a
> foreign accent and having neither beard, moustache nor
> whiskers, of a pale sallow complexion and rather fair I should
> think, entered the shop around 10 o'clock. He took a chain from
> his pocket, apparently not attached to his watch, and asked him
> if I would let him have a new Albert chain for it of about the
> same value. Although having a foreign accent, he spoke English
> so plainly that I perfectly understood him. He wanted to have a
> new chain, without having to pay any money, for the old one,
> which was of the best description of gold.

The transaction was then completed, and later, the new chain which
was pawned was identified by Death as the one he had given the young
man.

Evidently Muller had taken the duplicate to Annis's shop and
pawned it. Muller's lodgings were searched and, hidden in the chimney,
was a scrap of silk, such as might have come from a man's sleeve, with
blood on it. It was thought that Muller had used this to wipe
bloodstains from his shoes after the murder. Sir Richard Mayne,
Commissioner of the Metropolitan Police, was told of this and realized
that Muller would need to be questioned about the murder. Therefore,
on the same day (20 July), Inspector Tanner, Mr Death and Matthews,
took a steamship, *The City of Manchester*, for New York. They took a
warrant for Muller's arrest with them. Because it was feared they might
not arrive before Muller, a second warrant was sent on a faster ship and

this warrant was endorsed by the American minister in London, as required by the extradition treaty.

More facts emerged about the top suspect. Muller had been born in Cologne in about 1839. On leaving school he was apprenticed to a gunsmith and came to London in 1862. He was unable to find work as a gunsmith, and eventually began working for Mr Hodgkinson as mentioned above. He also lived at the same house as a Mr Matthews and became engaged to his daughter. The engagement was broken off by early 1864. It was said that he was jealous and potentially violent. In appearance, he was five feet six, slender, with a pale complexion and light brown hair. He lacked whiskers or a moustache.

Apparently on the evening of the murder, Muller had spent some time with Elizabeth Repsch, the wife of a German tailor of Jewry Street, Aldgate. She was with him until 7.30 pm, when she left him in Haffa's company. He had not then spoken of any overseas journey. By 8.30, when she returned, Muller was gone. She next saw him on Monday morning, shortly after he had exchanged the old watch chain for a new one. He claimed to have bought both the watch and a ring, which he then showed her and Haffa, from a man at the docks, while enquiring about a passage to America (this man, assuming he ever existed, was never located). He was also wearing a new hat; Muller claimed he had damaged the old one and thrown it away. Elizabeth thought the hat found in the railway compartment was the same as the one Muller used to wear, but was not entirely certain. She never saw Muller again after 14 July.

Haffa could shed more light on Muller's movements. When Muller left him, he said he 'was going to see his girl, his sweetheart', in Camberwell. This was about 7.45.

This murder excited a great deal of public interest, even more so than murder usually did at this time. Perhaps not until the Jack the Ripper murders of 1888 did the press give a killing so much attention.

Muller arrived at New York on 24 August. Inspectors Kerressey and Tanner, with Death, had arrived before him; just as Chief Inspector Dew was to arrive before Crippen in 1910. Muller was arrested and identified. When he was brought before the City Marshal, he told him that he was innocent and could prove it. He was remanded and the extradition process began. His captors searched his belongings and found the hat and watch which seemed to prove his guilt.

Muller was escorted back to England on the *Etna*, arriving on 17

September at Liverpool. The boat was met by a steam tug, and angry crowds waited for him by the docks. Muller was taken by cab to a police station. It was alleged 'The excitement in the town from the time *Etna* came in sight was very great, and it increased as he was being conveyed to the police office.' Muller himself 'appeared very unconcerned' and had not spoken of the murder on his return voyage. He was taken by train to London and on arrival at Euston met a large crowd. He was committed for trial at the Bow Street Magistrates' court on the following day.

This murder case was described by Charles Dickens as one of the two great sensations of the time; the other being a commercial crisis. Those who know the novelist through his books as a liberal humanitarian might be interested in his comment on the case before the trial, when he wrote thus, in a letter to a friend:

> I hope that the gentleman [Muller] will be hanged, and have hardly a doubt of it, though croakers contrariwise are not wanting. It is difficult to conceive any other line of defence than that the circumstances proved, taken separately, are slight. But a sound Judge will immediately charge the jury that the strength of the circumstances lies in their being put together and will thread them together on a fatal rope.

Muller's trial at the Old Bailey took three days (27–29 October). The court room was packed to capacity, such was the public interest in the case. As expected, the main witnesses for the prosecution were Matthews and Death, who attested, respectively, to the hat found at the murder scene being Muller's and the fact that he had sold Briggs's watch chain to the jeweller. Yet there was the evidence of Lee to contend with; for he had seen two other men with Briggs in the railway compartment just before the train was about to depart and he thought that neither man there was Muller. But there was new evidence, too. On the night of the murder, Muller had told Haffa at 7.45 at Old Jewry that he was going to Camberwell. Apparently, according to Elizabeth Jones, Muller came to her house, which was a brothel, incidentally, at St George's Road, Peckham. He had come to see one of her girls, a Mary Ann Eldred. Perhaps unfortunately for Muller, she had left the house at 9 pm. The clock gave the time as 9.30 pm, and Mrs Jones remembered it because that was when a telegram arrived for her. If this was true, then Muller could hardly have caught the same train as Briggs, because it would have taken him more than 20 minutes to reach Fenchurch Street station. The Camberwell omnibus which Muller could have caught did not travel through Peckham until 9.55 and did not arrive at King William Street until 10.20. Therefore, Muller must be innocent. Furthermore, Miss Eldred said that Muller had spoken to her before the murder of going to America. The prosecutors did not let these witnesses speak without challenging them. In particular, they cast doubts on the reliability of Mrs Jones and the accuracy of her clock. Perhaps Muller did go there, but if he set off at 7.45, he could have gone there, found his friend was not there, and returned in time to arrive at Fenchurch Street at 9.45. Lee's testimony to seeing two men in the carriage was also questioned and it was believed that Lee was mistaken as to which night he saw Briggs there. The jury believed the prosecutors' version of events and, after a mere 15 minutes, found Muller guilty of murder.

Muller himself was allowed to speak. He said, in his broken English, 'I wish to say I am satisfied with my trial. I know I have been convict by your law, but not upon the statement – by false.' A witness later wrote, 'these last words of Muller's struck me so very forcibly as containing no denial of guilt, or assertion of active innocence'.

There was doubt among some as to whether Muller was indeed guilty. There was a penny pamphlet, *Who murdered Mr Briggs?* published. The writer stated, 'The object of my pamphlet is to show that he [Muller] did not, or at least that Muller alone, is not guilty'. He argued that the evidence against Muller was circumstantial. For instance, the hat that was meant to be his, could have fitted many other men. James Smith wrote a similar pamphlet, titled, *Has Muller been tried?*

Muller returned to Newgate to await execution. His counsel, Thomas Beard, came to see him at once and had a conversation with his client, in the presence of the prison governor, Mr Jones. Muller was told that the fight to save his life would continue, and that the German Legal Protection Society, who had financed his defence, would continue to help him, in finding new evidence and presenting a memorial to the Home Secretary on his behalf.

After his first paroxysm of grief, Muller was quiet and composed, sleeping well. He spent much of his time reading and spoke but little to the warders. He had no visitors, except Mr Walbaum, a German

Lutheran chaplain in London, and Mr Davis, the prison chaplain.

Muller also came under suspicion of another recent murder – a not uncommon circumstance for convicted killers. In 1863, Emma Jackson had been killed in the St Giles district of London, having been stabbed by an unknown young man (the case is detailed in the author's *Unsolved Murders in Victorian and Edwardian London*). Among the suspects were German sugar bakers in Peckham. It was thought that a handkerchief belonging to the victim had been found in Muller's hat box. Yet the two witnesses who saw Emma with a man shortly before her death did not think Muller was the same man.

However, although cleared of that crime, his defenders had no luck with their memorial to Sir George Grey, the Home Secretary, which they had presented on 10 November. They argued that the evidence used to convict Muller was weak and, furthermore, they had new evidence to cast doubt on the conviction. First, on the night of the murder, a man with bloodstained clothes (not Muller) had been seen in Hackney, near to where Briggs had been found. Secondly, Ellen Blyth said she remembered that Muller had been wearing the same clothes on the day of the murder and on the following day. On the latter, there were no bloodstains, nor did it seem that any had been washed off. It was also argued that a small man such as Muller could not possibly have successfully assaulted a larger man, such as Briggs. But their pleas were in vain. Indeed, they actually annoyed some Germans resident in London, one of whom wrote, 'Most of the Germans in my acquaintance are fully convinced of the justness of the sentence against Muller.' He added that the German Legal Protection Society only represented a few Germans and that, if they did not like British justice, they could always return to Germany.

Meanwhile, preparations were being made for the execution of Muller. The scaffolding was being erected outside Newgate and the time for his death was announced. Crowds gathered and the roads nearby were blocked. Respectable people were shocked at these ruffianly and dirty people, numbering about 50,000, who were there for the spectacle. As *The Times* put it, 'Such a concourse as we hope may never again be assembled either for the spectacle which they had in view on for the gratification of such lawless ruffianism as yesterday found its scope around the gallows.' Just before he was taken to his death, Muller confessed to the chaplain that he had indeed killed Briggs, 'Ich habe es gethan'.

It is presumed that this was correct. Certainly Muller had the motive to kill a wealthy man who was alone, vulnerable and much older than he was. Briggs was probably taken by surprise as he was dozing on the train when he was suddenly attacked. Muller did have one of the dead man's possessions in his hands. And the hat found in the railway compartment was his. Therefore, presumably Lee was mistaken, as was Mrs Jones and her clock which told the wrong time. Yet without the final confession, there would have remained a great deal of doubt over the justness of the verdict and execution.

After the murder, there were calls for improved safety measures on trains. An Act of Parliament of 1868 made it compulsory for all passenger trains to install a system of alarms. The earliest alarm systems were unreliable, easy to tamper with and often useless, as Rebecca Dickinson discovered in 1875 (see Chapter 4). However, with time they became more efficient. South Western trains went further and installed peepholes, or 'Muller holes' in their railway compartments, but these were not universally popular for they reduced the privacy of the travelling public.

A final comment: in the opening chapter of *A Study in Scarlet*, Holmes refers to a number of criminals; one being 'the notorious Muller'. Could this be a reference to the killer here?

4

An Officer, But Not a Gentleman? 1875

'One feels so shocked and so shamed as a gentleman
being capable of such a thing'

Most of those involved in real crime, whether as victim, perpetrator or
investigator are usually of humble status, despite fictional depictions of
wrongdoing. This account of a misdeed on board a train in the middle
of Victoria's reign concerns people of a more exalted social status.

It was Thursday afternoon of 17 June 1875 and a young woman was
being seen off from Midhurst station by her two sisters and widowed
mother. It was 3 o'clock. She was Miss Rebecca Kate Dickinson, aged
22, and was fortunate to be both good-looking and of comfortable
upper middle-class stock. Since September 1874 she had lived with her
family at Dunsford, near Midhurst, Sussex. Prior to that they had
resided at New Park, Lymington, until her father's death. The family
was well off, with her father William leaving nearly £60,000 in his will.
Her brothers included a doctor of Chesterfield Street, a captain in the
Royal Engineers and a barrister in Chancery. She was travelling to
London to meet her married sister and her brother-in-law, one
Bagshawe, prior to the three of them departing to Switzerland for a
three-week holiday. Her labelled luggage, consisting of three cases and
a portmanteau, were loaded into the same compartment.

She sat alone in a first class compartment, facing the direction of
travel. Nothing happened until the next station stop, which was
Petersfield. Here she changed trains to take the Portsmouth to London
South Western train. The train had a corridor, so there were two exits
from the compartment. At Liphook station, a middle-aged man entered
the compartment and sat in the opposite corner to Miss Dickinson. He
was a complete stranger to her.

For most of what happened next, we have only Miss Dickinson's account. Certainly all began ordinarily enough. The window was down and the man asked her if she minded the draught and she said she did not. There was no more conversation between the two until they passed Hazelmere. Then the man began to expound on the beauty of the countryside through which they were passing. He got up from his seat and sat opposite Miss Dickinson. He then talked about Aldershot and she said that she had a brother there and had been to a steeplechase ball there, too.

Conversation proceeded on conventional lines. Miss Dickinson later reported:

> He next talked about pictures at the Royal Academy, and the conversation then turned upon Midhurst, from which town I told him I came. He told me he was on the staff at Aldershot, and was then stationed at the North Camp. He looked at the labels on my luggage, and asked me if I was going to Dover that night. I replied that I should be off the following morning.

The man asked if she was travelling alone and she mentioned her two travelling companions. He told her she would have to wait two hours at Waterloo and suggested she remain in London for a few days. She replied that she had recently spent a fortnight in the capital and the conversation then turned to matters theatrical. They talked about a recent production of *Hamlet* and then about mesmerism.

By now the train had reached Woking (11 minutes late), the last station the train was designated to stop at before reaching Clapham. It was then, just before 5pm, that the man began to move onto more personal matters. He asked when she would next be travelling on the same route. The following dialogue ensued.

'No.'

'You won't?'

The man pulled the window up.

'Will you give me your name?'

'I shan't.'

'Why not?'

'Because I don't choose; I don't see any reason why I should.'

The man asked her what her Christian name was and she refused to answer. He then sat next to her, taking hold of her hand. This prompted the following response.

'Get away, I won't have you sitting here.'

She pushed him away, but to no avail. He grabbed her around the waist with one hand and kissed her, declaring: 'You must kiss me darling.'

She got up and went to ring the communication cord. He implored her not to, but she ignored him and rang it. It produced no effect for it was not working. He forced her back into the corner and kissed her again. She said: 'If I tell you my name, will you get off?'

Then, according to her:

> I don't think he made any reply, but he sank down close in front
> of me, and I felt his hand underneath my dress, on my stocking,
> above my boot. I got up instantly and pushed the window with
> my elbow to see if I could break the glass. Finding I could not
> do that, I got the window down, and put my head and elbows
> out. I screamed and nobody heard.

She then felt quite strangled by her assailant, who was pulling her back. She screamed and then turned the handle of the door, opening it and stepping out onto the footboard. With one hand she held onto the door handle and he held her by the other. She now faced a new peril and said, 'If you leave go, I shall fall.'

'Get in dear! Get in dear! You get in and I will get out of the other door.' But the other door had been locked at Guildford. However, other passengers were now looking out of their windows and were seeing her plight. She saw two men, and asked,

'How long is it before the train stops?'

'I don't know'.

George Burnett was one of the men who saw her. He had boarded the train at Guildford and recalled hearing a scream after the train had passed through Weybridge. He was concerned that she might be killed by falling from the train.

Henry Bailey, the guard, also saw her. The train was now passing Esher, near the old paper mills. The driver also witnessed what was happening and blew the whistle. Bailey applied the brake.

After about five miles of travel, the train, which was travelling at between 40 and 45 mph, stopped. The train had now reached Esher. Before it had done so, her hat flew off, near Walton station. As it did, her assailant implored her thus: 'Don't say anything; you don't know what trouble you will get me into; say you were frightened.'

She did not reply. When other passengers arrived to see what the trouble was, she replied: 'That man would not leave me alone.'

Miss Dickinson's dress was disarranged. Bailey asked the man what had happened and he replied: 'I have been doing nothing. I know her brother at Aldershot.'

Bailey noticed that only one of the man's trouser buttons had been fastened – a point which might be of great importance in ascertaining his intentions towards Miss Dickinson. Mr Pike, a businessman, also noticed this, and that the man's clothing was in a state of disarray. The man, who scribbled down his name and address for the guard, then had to spend the remainder of the journey in the company of some other men (including Burnett), while the young lady travelled with the Revd James Brown, minister of an Independent chapel in Brixton (like Burnett, he had been alarmed by the sight of Miss Dickinson hanging out of the train). Brown recalled 'she was very much alarmed, but still very much possessed'. The man requested to leave at Vauxhall, but was told he must not.

On arrival at Waterloo, they went to the superintendent's office, being escorted by William Atter, a railway policeman. Her assailant was also taken there and was now very contrite:

'I am very sorry if anything I did frightened you. I know your brother very well indeed; give me his address and I will write to him.'

'You may do what you choose.'

Miss Dickinson gave her name and address to the officials present, but did not give any information to her assailant. Accompanied by the clergyman, she went to her brother's house in Chesterfield Street.

Her assailant was detained. It was then that his identity became known. He was Colonel Valentine Baker. He had been born in Enfield in 1827, the son of a wealthy man. Baker bought a commission in the 10th Hussars in 1848. He had had a varied military career, serving in South Africa, the Crimea, Ireland and India, in both the Hussars and the Lancers. By 1865, he was a colonel and was a good officer, interested in both the theory of war and his men's welfare. In 1865 he married and became a father to two children. He also became a friend of the Prince of Wales and gained an important contact with the Duke of Cambridge, commander in chief of the army. However, with the return of his regiment to England in 1872, he resigned his commission and, after an expedition in Asia, took a staff post at Aldershot in 1874. As assistant quartermaster general, he was told to supervise a great military review, to take place in August 1875. This, then, was the man who travelled up to London to dine with the Duke of Cambridge on 17 June 1875 and met Miss Dickinson en route.

Baker was very apologetic: 'I am sorry I did it; I don't know what possessed me to do it, I being a married man.'

Baker was arrested by the Surrey police on the following day and on Saturday 19 June he appeared before the County Bench at Guildford. He was charged with indecent assault on Miss Dickinson. In the packed court room were Mr Poland for the prosecution and Mr Lilley for the defence. The latter asked that the hearing be postponed for a week to allow him time to prepare the defence, as he had only just received his brief. Poland said he would be happy for this to occur, or for the hearing to proceed. After some discussion, the magistrates agreed to Lilley's suggestion and Baker was bailed for £500.

When the hearing occurred, on 24 June, the witnesses told the court what they had seen. The defence would be reserved, it was announced. Baker then said he wanted to make a statement. This was an unusual request, but it was granted. He said:

> I am placed here in a most delicate and difficult position. If any act of mine on the occasion referred to could have given any annoyance to Miss Dickinson, I beg to express to her my most unqualified regret. At the same time, I solemnly declare, upon my honour, that the case was not as it has been presented today by her under the influence of exaggerated fear and unnecessary alarm. To the evidence of the police constable Atter, I give the most unqualified denial. I may add that I don't intend in the least to say that she wilfully misrepresented the case, but I say that she has represented it incorrectly, no doubt under the influence of exaggerated fear and unnecessary alarm.

Baker was bailed for £4,000. There was no shortage of men who were willing to stand sureties for him. His brother Samuel and a fellow officer were happy to do so. He was then committed for trial.

At Surrey Assizes, held at Croydon on 2 August, Baker was tried for both attempted rape and the lesser charge of indecent assault. The case had shocked the nation. Not only had a terrible act taken place and another, even more heinous one been allegedly attempted, but the victim was a young and innocent woman and the perpetrator an officer and a gentleman. Most people had already decided, in their moral outrage, that Baker was guilty. There was therefore a great deal of excitement about the trial and on the day itself, the court room and the street outside was packed with people of both sexes, long before the trial began. It is unclear whether the crowd were good natured or not.

Baker pleaded not guilty. The prosecution outlined the case against him; that is, he had talked to Miss Dickinson on the train and then kissed her and had then tried to assault her after Woking. Miss Dickinson told the court her version of events, followed by the other witnesses, giving the same versions that had already been related. The defence could not draw on any witnesses to testify to Baker's innocence, and the accused himself could not speak on his own behalf (a legal position that changed in 1907). It was stated that Miss Dickinson merely said that she had been insulted and had not accused Baker of the charges that were now laid against him. He also suggested that it would have been an act of madness to attack a woman who was about to meet other people. Fellow officers spoke of Baker's valour and ability as a soldier.

However, although Baker was found innocent of attempted rape, he was deemed guilty of indecent assault by the jury after only a short discussion. He was cashiered from the army, fined £500 and was sentenced to imprisonment in Horsemonger gaol for a year, though without hard labour. He had to be secretly removed from the court and over 50 policemen had to be present to control the crowd. Newspapers covered the trial in great detail; the *Daily Telegraph* devoted nine columns to it and the *Evening Standard* had the news of the case transmitted by the expensive and unusual method of telegraph. Such was the popularity of evening newspapers covering the case that they doubled in price.

The Queen herself took an interest in the case, writing to one of her daughters, Louisa, Crown Princess of Prussia, on 11 August:

> that awful trial of Colonel Valentine Baker! Was there ever such a thing and such a position for a poor young girl? And what a disgrace to the Army. No punishment is severe enough . . . She is a very nice girl – though some officers and people tried to excuse him by abusing the poor unprotected girl. But the country was furious with him and he will be disgraced for life . . . What is to happen if officers, high in position, behave as none of the lowest would have dared to do unless a severe example is

made . . . Colonel Baker has a very bad moral character.

Her daughter replied that the case had not made the foreign press, and wrote that it was 'most distressing and makes one shudder, it is terrible to think what a slur such conduct throws on a whole existence – and one feels so shocked and shamed at a gentleman being capable of such a thing'.

Yet many people stood by him, including family and friends, the Prince of Wales and fellow officers. In 1876, he served with the Turks and, in the 1880s, with the Egyptian police, where he reorganized their gendarmerie. He also saw active service in the Sudan against the Mahdists, where he was wounded. In 1887, there was a chance that he would be reinstated, but he died that year. However, it seemed that by now he had redeemed himself; being buried with full military honours in Cairo and being praised by senior colleagues. According to *The Times*, 'his career . . . might have been among the most brilliant in our service . . . [but for] the error which deprived his country of his services' and referred to 'the splendid atonement which he sought to make'.

It is presumed that Baker was guilty of trying to assault Miss Dickinson. Why he did so is unclear. Nothing in his character leads one to suppose he was naturally violent towards women. It can only be concluded that, finding himself alone with an attractive young woman, an overmastering passion consumed him and this led him to assault Miss Dickinson, who was struck with such terror that she risked her life in trying to escape from him by attempting to leave the train whilst it was in transit. He certainly paid the price for his moment of folly.

Other crimes of this type occurred later in the century; a woman was attacked in 1887 on a train between Shrewsbury and Wellington; two were attacked in 1892, one on the London–Brighton line and another on the Midland one. In all cases, the victims escaped by leaving the compartment whilst the train was in transit, one taking the dangerous expedient of clambering onto the roof.

5

The Murder on the Brighton Railway, 1881

'I am glad you found me. I am sick of it.
I should have given myself up in a day or two.'

Frederick Isaac Gold was born in about 1818 in London. He had been a corn merchant for most of his life, residing at Wentworth Place, Mile End Road. Gold retired from the profession in 1863. However, he was still involved in business matters and owned a freehold baker's shop on East Street, Walworth, in south London. The shop was kept for Gold's nephew. Gold was also a married man, though he and his wife, Lydia Matilda, had no children. The couple had lived at Titchfield Preston, near Brighton, since at least 1871, when they had but one servant. Gold was in very good health, had a robust constitution and was of temperate habits. He usually had with him about two or three sovereigns. He also had an old-fashioned gold watch and chain which were hung about his neck. In 1881 he was worth £1,670 9s 1d, a fair sum.

As he did every Monday morning, Gold went up to London. He went on other days, too, but on Mondays he was a regular commuter to London. Monday 27 June 1881 was no exception. As his wife later related, 'He left home at five minutes past eight in the morning, with the intention of going by train to Brighton, in order to catch the up express train leaving Brighton at 8.45.' Arriving at London Bridge station, he then went to his shop and collected the previous week's takings from Mrs Cross, amounting to £38 5s 1d, putting it into a small bag. This money was then paid into the eastern branch of the London and Westminster Bank and then Gold went back to the station to catch the train home. He usually took about £10 for housekeeping expenses for the forthcoming week, too. However, it seems that no one was aware that he was carrying any money, except his wife and their servant.

On boarding the 2 pm express train at London Bridge, Gold, as was usual, chose a compartment in which he would be alone. His wife remarked of this habit, 'he never liked getting into a full compartment. He was a man of not very conversational mood, and used often to say that it confused him if people talked to him too much. He had a habit of closing his eyes and lying back in the seat as if asleep, in order that people should not talk to him.' Humphrey Gibson, a chemist of King's Road, Brighton, was also on board, though in a second class compartment.

The journey was not an ordinary one. After leaving London Bridge, the first stop was Croydon. Ann Brown, wife of Daniel Brown, a farm labourer, had a cottage in Horley 100 yards from the railway line on which the train passed between 2 and 3 pm. She later said, 'It was going fast. I saw in one of the carriages two gentlemen standing up. They appeared to be fighting or "larking".' The next stop was at Preston Park, where Gibson noticed that blood was flowing from the compartment which had been used by Gold. It was at this point that Gibson recalled that he had heard what he had thought to be the sound of blasts from a fog horn. These had been emitted in Mertsham tunnel. Might they not have been gun shots?

Later, the train had passed through Balcombe tunnel. About an hour later, Thomas Jennings, a Horley labourer employed by the railway company, was walking through that same tunnel, with his nephew, William. It was about 4.15 pm. The two made a shocking discovery, as Jennings senior later remarked: 'In the middle of the tunnel I saw the body of a man lying in the six foot between the two roads. The head was lying towards the south and the body was lying parallel with the line. The body was lying on the back. It was dark but I had a light.'

Jennings felt the body. It was still warm. He also noticed that it was clothed and bloody. He then took the corpse to Balcombe station and from there it was removed to the stables of the Railway Inn. The body had not been in the tunnel for long, because John Jennings, a ganger of platelayers, had passed through the tunnel shortly before 3 pm that afternoon, and he had noticed nothing remarkable. The 2 pm London to Brighton train had passed through the three-quarter-mile-long tunnel shortly afterwards. Clearly the victim had travelled, when alive, on that same train, and had either jumped out of the train or had been pushed.

On the train reaching Preston Park, the next stop after Croydon, a strange and shocking sight greeted those on the platform. This was a young man, but he hardly presented a conventional appearance. Apparently, 'His face was otherwise pale, and there were marks of blood upon it and blood upon his neck. There was dried blood on each nostril.

The man looked weak, but was perfectly composed and answered questions rationally.' He lacked a collar and neck tie and wore a frock coat and grey trousers. His trousers and coat were bloodstained. Hardly an ordinary-looking sight. Station staff thought he might have been a lunatic who had tried to injure himself. His name was Percy Lefroy Mapleton.

Mapleton had been born in Peckham in about 1860. It appears he was an orphan, for in the following year he was living with the family of his elderly uncle in Deptford. In 1881 he lived with his cousin in Cathcart Road, Wallington, which was also used as a boarding school. He had no fixed employment and had very little money. He had tried his hand at writing, but his output was not of a high standard.

The young man's story was a shocking one. He had been travelling from London Bridge and said that his companions were an elderly gentleman and a man who looked like a countryman, middle-aged and bewhiskered. The train entered the Merstham tunnel and a shot rang out. Someone then knocked Mapleton on the head and he fell unconscious, not awakening until the train arrived at Preston Park. He said to Thomas Watson, the guard, 'I have been cruelly treated on the way by two other passengers who were in the same compartment and who left the train on the way down.' Hanging from his pocket was a watch chain – not the safest place to put so valuable an item, as Watson commented. The compartment in which Mapleton had been travelling was smeared with blood, but there was no sign of anybody else, alive nor dead. The stationmaster sent a man to Brighton station to give them the news.

Mapleton and Richard Gibson, the platform inspector, went to Brighton town hall to report the matter to the police, where he saw Chief Constable Terry, then to Sussex Hospital. Benjamin Hall was the acting house surgeon and saw to Mapleton's injuries. He had suffered a number of minor wounds. These included a small cut on his forehead, one above his ear and six minor injuries to his scalp. His hands, face and neck were smeared with dry blood. Hall dressed the wounds. He later observed, 'They were very peculiar wounds; I have never seen anything like them.' They were not caused by gravel thrown up by the train, nor by shots. Oddly enough, Mapleton told him that he had been shot at, but generally speaking was reticent as to what exactly had happened. Hall was uncertain how the wounds had been caused; they could even have been self-inflicted. He added, 'The patient was unwilling to stay, although for his own sake, I thought it was advisable that he should do so.' To this Mapleton replied, 'I cannot; I have an engagement in town which I must keep.'

Mapleton then left the hospital and was taken to the police station again. En route, he stopped to buy a collar and a tie. The police were becoming suspicious of Mapleton and had him searched. Apart from a few small coins, they also found some Hanoverian coins of higher value. Yet there were no grounds on which he could be detained, so he was allowed to leave, albeit in the company of a detective sergeant who had been loaned by the Met to the railway company; the man's name was George Holmes (the first Sherlock Holmes novel was actually set in 1881).

Holmes was to accompany Mapleton to Croydon. They took the 6.10 train from Brighton. At Three Bridges, the stationmaster told him of the discovery of the corpse. Mapleton looked uneasy when he heard the news. At Croydon, they took a cab to Wallington. When they arrived, Mapleton said that he wanted to change into clean clothes, the ones he was wearing being bloody. Holmes saw nothing wrong in letting him do so. Mapleton and Holmes arrived at Cathcart Road, Wallington, where Mapleton lived, at 9.30 pm. After waiting in the drawing room for a time, Holmes discovered that his quarry had left through the back entrance, telling his cousin that he had gone to see a doctor.

It was believed by the police that Mapleton had gone to London and that his arrest was imminent. A poster was issued in order to assist in this. It read as follows:

> Wanted, for murder, Arthur Mapleton, alias Lefroy, aged 22, five feet eight, very thin, hair dark and short, small dark whiskers and moustache. He was last seen at Wallington about 9.30 last night (Monday) and was then dressed in a dark coat, supposed with a low black hat, worn at the back of the head. He has had scratches at his throat and supposed to be wounded in the head. Wears a gold open faced watch, no. 16, 261, maker Griffiths, Mile End Road.

Mapleton was at large for some days. On the day after the murder he went to Islington, where he borrowed 15s from a relative who was unaware that he was a wanted man.

Meanwhile, in Preston, Mrs Gold knew her husband's habits of old. He normally returned home at 3.30 pm. On this day he did not do so. She then assumed he would return by the 6.15 train. Again, he did not. It was then that she became alarmed, 'about ten minutes past eight I went up to Preston station, saw Mr Hall, the stationmaster, and asked him whether there had been an accident'. Hall assured her that he had heard no such news, so she assumed her husband had been detained in London by business. But he did not arrive by the next train, either.

She returned home and there eventually received the devastating news. 'At five minutes past ten I received a telegram from the stationmaster at Balcombe, addressed to Titchfield, Preston. It stated, "Man found dead this afternoon in tunnel. On him name of James F. Gold. He is now lying here. Reply quick"'. After discussing what best to do with a neighbour, Mrs Gold took a late train to Balcombe. Mr Lee Hollis of Clermont Road, Preston, and assistant to a wine merchant, and who had known the Golds for ten years, accompanied her. On arrival at Balcombe station, the stationmaster advised her not to view the body. Hollis did so, and he confirmed it was that of Mrs Gold's husband.

On the following day, the corpse was examined by Dr Thomas Spry Byass, who practised at Cuckfield. His initial impressions were thus, 'The face and hands are covered in dirt and blackened. The right hand is clenched, the left relaxed. The clothes are saturated with blood – more on the right wristband of the shirt than on the left'. The clothes were intact. All, except the socks, were bloody. There was a wound on the right hand between the thumb and first finger. This had probably been caused by a knife and was as deep as the bone. There were also scratches on the hand and all over the body. There was a knife wound along the throat, but it was not a deep one, perhaps caused by something bigger than a penknife and smaller than a carving knife.

He was convinced that the wounds were not caused by the body being thrown from the train or dragged along the tracks. Death was due to haemorrhage to the brain caused by the numerous wounds to the head. Dr Byass was asked if Gold had been shot but he stated that there was no evidence of any bullet wounds. Some injuries took place after death, but he could not differentiate between them. Benjamin Hall examined the body and noted the fractures to the head. These would have caused death, he said but only after about 15 minutes.

The inquest commenced at 9 am at Balcombe on Wednesday 29 June. Mr Wynne E Baxter was the coroner and it seems to have been a high-profile affair. Solicitors for the railway company and for Mrs Gold attended, as did Inspector Turpin. As usual at this time, the jury had the unpleasant task of viewing the corpse in the stables of the Railway Inn, which they did, as well as seeing the compartment where the killing took place. Hollis identified the body.

Baxter questioned Hollis and Mrs Gold. He was particularly interested in any relatives she might have had in Croydon. Apparently her sister married one Alfred Peel, a former businessman, and they lived in Wallington. Gold had not seen them for some time. Baxter also asked where Gold's brother lived and, again, she did not know the answer. Miss Mary Peel confirmed that Gold had not visited them on the day of his death or on any other recent day. It seemed that Mapleton might have formed a great impression of Gold's wealth through Mrs Peel.

The railway compartment which Gold had travelled down in was examined. There were bloodstains on the upholstery of the seating and also on the floor. A piece of lead which was once a bullet was found embedded into the wall. An attempt had been made to extract this. Three bullet holes were also found. The clothes of the deceased and some of Mapleton's were also shown to the jury. Both sets were much bloodstained. The train compartments were fitted with an electric communication cord, and this was found to have been in working order, but it had not been pulled on that fatal journey. They also found six Hanoverian coins of the same type as found on Mapleton.

When the inquest was resumed on 7 July, there was more medical evidence. This time Dr Thomas Bond, senior police surgeon (and who was to be involved in some of the inquests of Jack the Ripper's victims in 1888), was the physician called upon to deliver it. Contrary to his colleague's report, he found that Gold had been shot as well as knifed and these wounds had not been self-inflicted. The coroner summed up: Mapleton, an impoverished young man, entered the train with the intent to rob, and finding Gold, shot and stabbed him. Thus the inquest was concluded; the verdict being that this was a case of murder committed by Mapleton. Superintendent Berry of East Grinstead was given a warrant for his arrest.

Mapleton was on the run for some days. Eventually, on the evening of Friday 8 July, the police caught up with him, following an anonymous tip off. Inspectors Donald Swanson (who was to play a part in the Ripper investigations, later suggesting that Aaron Kosminski was the notorious murderer) and Frederick Smith of the CID, paid a visit to Smith Street, Stepney. According to Swanson:

> At a quarter to 8 o'clock on Friday night in company with Inspector Jarvis and Police Constable Hopkins, I went to 32 Smith Street, Stepney. On entering the front room on the first floor, I saw the prisoner, Percy Lefroy Mapleton, sitting in an armchair. Addressing him I said, 'Percy Lefroy Mapleton?' In reply, he said, 'Yes, I expected it'. I told him I was a police officer and that I should apprehend him on a charge of wilfully murdering Mr Gold on the Brighton Railway on 27 June. In answer he said, 'I am not obliged to make any reply, and I think it

better not to make any answer'. I wrote it in my pocket book as he said it, and read it over to him. In reply to that, he said, 'I will qualify that by saying I am not guilty'. No further conversation occurred and I took him back to Scotland Yard.

Mapleton was searched, as was the room. He had only one shilling on his person, but some of his clothes had bloodstains on them. Mapleton told the policemen, 'I am glad you found me. I am sick of it. I should have given myself up in a day or two. I have regretted it ever since I ran away. It puts a different complexion on the case, but I could not bear the exposure.' He then asked if he could see a lawyer and was told that he could. He was then taken to Lewes gaol by train; crowds gathered at various stations in order to try and catch a glimpse of such a notorious personality. At Hayward's Heath, where they had to change trains, the crowds shouted abuse at him. En route he had been chatting and smoking with his captors, excited when passing through the same tunnels as he had thirteen days ago, and then rather depressed. He arrived at the gaol at 10.30.

After Mapleton's disappearance he had initially gone to his sister's house in Liverpool Road, Islington. He then went to Smith Street, on 30 June, explaining that he was an engraver and needed peace and quiet. He had called himself Mr Park and said that he was from Liverpool. The landlady, Mrs Bickers, was unsuspecting and did not read the newspapers. He had paid her 6s a week and a deposit of 3s 6d, and had not gone out in the daytime until his arrest.

The trial at the Maidstone Assizes took place on 4–8 November. Mapleton pleaded not guilty. Yet evidence of his guilt was strong. On 21 June, at Mr Creek's pawnbrokers on High Street, Borough, the assistant Mr Adams had been pledged a small revolver. The young man who had pledged the weapon gave his name as William Lee, of Southampton Street, Peckham. Between 11 and 12 on 27 June, the same man redeemed the weapon. When Adams was shown a number of men in Lewes Gaol, he was able to identity 'William Lee', who was none other than Mapleton. Mapleton could have easily have reached London from Wallington by train, catching the 10.49, reaching there at 11.20, or the 11.23, arriving at 11.53.

He had also defrauded a shopkeeper earlier on the day of the murder. He was in debt to one Mr Ellis, a Croydon stationer, to the tune of £1 7s 6d. In order to meet this debt, on the morning of the murder, he gave Ellis's assistant two Hanoverian medals which he pretended were sovereigns (gold coins worth £1 each), and took 13s 6d in exchange.

There was much evidence to show that Mapleton was deeply in debt. He had on his person, when arrested, a number of pawnbrokers' tickets. He had pawned coats and his watch as well as the aforesaid gun.

Mapleton was found to be a liar. He told the police that the reason for his visit to Brighton was to see one Mrs Nye-Chart, lessee of Brighton theatre. She did not know of him and was unaware of any reason why he would have business with her.

Mapleton's defence was that there was no reason why he would know Gold had much money with him, because he did not know him. They also said that Gold was a powerfully built man and that a puny specimen such as Mapleton could not have overpowered him. Finally, why should Mapleton commit one felony in the morning and then murder in the afternoon? It was also stated that the real killer was the third man who Mapleton declared was in the same carriage as he and Gold, and that this unknown man could have left the train as it slowed down before arriving at the station where Mapleton alighted.

Yet the jury was unconvinced and retired for a mere ten minutes before declaring their verdict. He was found guilty and sentenced to death. Mapleton dramatically declared in court, 'The day will come when you will know that you have murdered me.' Meanwhile, he was returned to Lewes gaol, accompanied by two warders on a train from Maidstone, which was half an hour late. His family and friends presented a memorial to the Home Secretary to plead for a reprieve, on the grounds of insanity, and that he should therefore have been sent to Broadmoor. To strengthen this case, Mapleton confessed to the murder of one Lieutenant Roper at Chatham Barracks on 11 February 1881. A relative, Mrs Clayton, visited him in prison.

On 24 November, the murder weapon was found, quite by chance. A platelayer was working on the Brighton line and found the pistol. It was a four-shooter and was identified by the pawnbroker as that pledged by Mapleton on 21 June and redeemed on 27 June. This evidence was not necessary, but it neatly rounded off the case. The memorial in favour of the condemned man was turned down and his confession to the previous murder was seen as merely a fabrication. The end came on 29 November and, inside Lewes gaol, Mapleton was hanged. Despite the fact there was once great interest in his fate, very few people bothered to turn up outside the prison at the time of the execution. In any case, all they would have seen was the raising of the black flag.

6

Murder of a Farmer, 1901

'I do not know what I did it for. I must have been mad. I had no cause.'

Mrs Rhoda King was the middle-aged wife of Thomas, a printer employed in the Ordnance Survey Department at Southampton. They lived in Exmoor Road, Southampton, and both were aged 54 in 1901. On 17 January 1901, she took the train from Southampton to Waterloo on the London and South Western line (the same line as travelled by Rebecca Dickinson 26 years earlier) in order to visit her daughter-in-law, who lived in Battersea, and who was unwell. She boarded a third class compartment on the 11.15 from Southampton West, which was scheduled to arrive at Waterloo just after half past one. It should have been a most ordinary journey.

It was not to be. At the train's first stop, which was at Eastleigh, a well-built young man entered the compartment. Mrs King was impressed by his smart appearance, as he was so well dressed and tall. He had dark brown hair and grey/hazel eyes. They said few words to one another. The man was George Henry Parker, born on 8 November 1877 (and so now aged 23) at Studley, Warwickshire, and he was a former Royal Marine. Had Mrs King been very observant she might have noticed a tattoo on the back of his hand – a heart and anchor, with clasped hands.

The train made its next stop at Winchester at noon. William Pearson who appeared to be, as indeed he was, a prosperous middle-aged farmer (aged 45), then joined the other two. He sat opposite Mrs King, facing the engine. He lived at Christchurch Road, Winchester, and was married with two children. Well-known in local agricultural circles, he farmed Winnal Manor Farm, near Winchester. His brother was the vice chairman of Winchester Rural District Council. Pearson was travelling to London to cash a large cheque at a London bank.

None of the three knew each other. There was little conversation, either. However, Parker did ask Pearson for some money, but the latter refused him. Pearson read his newspaper and then began to doze. It was when the train was nearing its destination that the crisis of the day was to erupt. Mrs King later recalled:

> After passing Surbiton station, I turned my back to . . . [Parker] . . . to look out of the window, I had moved my seat to face the engine. About the time the train passed Surbiton . . . [Parker] . . . entered the lavatory chamber. I was standing up . . . just after he came out of the lavatory. Then I heard a 'bang' like a fog signal. I remember hearing two reports, and then I felt blood rushing down my face. Then I begged . . . [Parker] . . . not to do it again.

Parker had just shot both Pearson and Mrs King.

She exclaimed to Parker, 'My God! What have you done? Why did you do it?' 'I did it for money. I want some money. Do you have any?' Looking in her purse, she found a shilling and gave it to him. He took it and put it in his pocket.

It was only then that she looked at the other occupant of the compartment. Pearson was doubled up in the corner, and there was an ominous mark on his forehead. He had been shot dead. Parker held a smoking revolver. He then rifled through the dead man's clothes, taking his watch and chain, together with any money he could find, counting it and putting it away. Mrs King could stand no more of the unfolding horror. She screamed. Parker then turned towards her and threatened her with death unless she quietened down. He then threw a coin at her and said, 'Here is a sovereign; stop your noise.'

She said that it was of no use to her and she did not want it. Parker then said to her, 'I am sorry I shot you. I didn't mean to hurt you.' 'Why did you do it?' she answered. 'Well I wanted money. I was wicked, I know, but I couldn't help it. I am going to Liverpool tonight to start for South Africa and I wanted money.'

Parker must have put the gun down, for he then said, 'What have I done with that damned thing? I must not keep it about me. I have got a mind to put it in his hand and then they will think he did it himself.' 'If I were you, I would throw it out of the window.'

He looked out of the window, but saw some workmen there and they would see the act. Mrs King suggested, 'Wait till you get a little further on.'

He did so as the train was now beginning to slow down as it began to pull into Vauxhall. Flinging the revolver out of the window (it landed on the metals near Nine Elms Goods Yard – when it was found four of the six chambers were still loaded), Parker pushed Pearson's corpse to one side and opened the door of the compartment before the train had come to a stop. Before then, he had elicited a promise from Mrs King that she would not speak against him.

Once on platform 2, he moved quickly. He gave his ticket to Alfred Gibbons, the ticket collector. It was actually Pearson's. Doubtless to his distress, he heard Mrs King's voice behind him. She shouted, 'Stop that man – he has murdered someone in that carriage.' Meanwhile, Parker bolted down the stairs, followed by several porters. He managed to escape from the railway station and headed towards Vauxhall Bridge. Unfortunately for him, there was a police constable there on traffic control duty (PC Thomas Fuller). He joined in the chase. Parker realizing the bridge was blocked, ran towards the Southern Metropolitan Gas Works, over a small bridge over a creek in the yard and hid in a coke truck in the retort shed. His pursuers surrounded the shed. Fifteen minutes later, Parker could not stand the heat any longer and gave himself up. He was taken in a cab to Larkhall Lane Police Station, Clapham.

He was subsequently taken to Holloway prison; en route the crowd booed and yelled at him. When he was searched, he was found to have a purse with £5 in gold, a game licence and a leather cigar case, both of which had been stolen from Pearson. Apart from that, his belongings included a gun licence, dice, a pawnbroker's ticket for a watch and a soldier's discharge papers. He was charged with both murder and attempted murder.

More information was found out about Parker. He was the eldest of eight children, but aged 14 he had been sent to a reformatory. Later his parents split up, with his mother going to Birmingham to work in a cycle shop. He was a clerk until he joined the Royal Marine Artillery in London on 12 March 1896, perhaps because his brother was in the Royal Engineers. For the first three years in the service, both his character and ability were rated 'Good' or 'Very Good'. His conduct and his proficiency with weaponry was also highly rated. Yet in 1900 he was 'discharged with ignomiy', due to his being caught stealing. Enlisting again, later that year at Gosport, under the surname of Hill, his character was stated as 'Bad' and it was noticed that letters had been going missing from the barracks. It was found that Parker was the thief, trying to find money in his comrades' letters. He was arrested, discharged at the end of the year, and spent 21 days in prison. He then went to London, returning to Portsmouth with some jewellery and looking prosperous. He was suspected of having been involved in a jewellery theft at the Lyceum Theatre. He then disappeared. Apparently he had written to his father, saying he had a job as a barman.

He now wrote a letter to his father, trying to explain his actions: 'I do not know what I did it for. I must have been mad. I had no cause.' He explained that his father broke up the family home while his son was serving in the army and this had contributed to his son's current difficulties. Parker had other problems; he had spent £9 in Eastleigh and Southampton with a young woman from Portsmouth, who he now thought might kill herself. He wrote, 'But there is one girl in Portsmouth whom I love better than gold and she is not good looking. But I love her dearly and she does me. I promised that I would fetch her away from home next week and she is not happy there.'

The girl in question was Mrs Elizabeth Sarah Rowland, wife to a private soldier. Parker claimed to not know of her marital status. In the days prior to Parker's journey to London, the two went around together, spending money and going to the theatre. This resulted in Parker being left almost penniless. They said their farewells in Eastleigh on 17 January.

He also wrote to Mrs Pearson, expressing his regret and sorrow at his shooting her husband:

> I am really truly sorry and I feel for you and your husband's brother. I am truly sorry and repentant for having in an evil moment allowed myself to be carried away into committing the offence which I am now being charged . . . I had no intention of shooting your husband. No, none whatever. I purchased the revolver at Southampton with the intention of shooting the girl whom I have been going out with and myself. She was unhappy at home, and so was I. I shot your husband on the spur of the moment.

He denied ever asking Pearson for any money and said that Mrs King lied when she said otherwise. After begging her forgiveness, and God's, he went on to state that he deserved to die. He signed it 'The Wretched Murderer of your husband'.

Mrs King, meanwhile, was sent to the Beatrice Ward in St Thomas's Hospital. Her son, a quartermaster sergeant in the Royal Artillery based at Woolwich, later visited her. He was doubtless pleased to learn that she was making good progress. When her husband, a prominent freemason, heard that she had been shot, he had fainted at the news. The bullet had entered her left cheek and broke the jaw bone. However, it would not be a permanent injury and she later made a full recovery.

The inquest into Pearson's death began on 21 January at Lambeth Coroner's Court, presided over by Mr A Braxton Hicks. There was a crowd of 200–300 people outside the court, but Parker was not intimidated. Quite the reverse. He entered the court with head held high and a swinging gait. Sympathy was extended to the family of the deceased and to Mrs King. Due to her injury she could not be present at the hearing. James Pearson, one of the deceased's brothers, had identified the corpse at the mortuary. He had last seen his brother on 15 January. The court was adjourned until all the witnesses could be present. In the mean time, all the jurors were bound over for £40 to attend it. Pearson was buried at Winchester on the same day.

On 11 February the inquest was concluded. Parker briefly attended the court, though he did not wish to. Few people were aware of his being there, so he was not shouted at by anyone on his arrival or departure. There was important new evidence given. William Cox worked in a gunsmith's shop in Southampton. Between 10 and 11 on 17 January, he had sold a cheap revolver and ten cartridges for 7s 5d. A young man had bought them and Cox identified him as Parker by his photograph, but did not recognize the man himself when he arrived. He did not explain why he wanted the gun.

Dr Simpson of South Lambeth Road reported his findings from the post mortem. Death was due to the laceration of the brain, where the bullet had been found. The shot had been fired at very close range. The killer had fired on his victim whilst the former was standing and the latter was seated. Reference was made to the prisoner's letters which indicated his guilt. The jury concluded that this was murder and Parker was responsible. He was committed to trial at the Old Bailey by coroner's warrant. There he was found guilty and sentenced to hang. Parker was resigned to his fate.

Parker was hanged at 9 am on 19 March at Wandsworth Prison. The executioners were James and Thomas Billington. As Revd Phipps the prison chaplain said, Parker maintained to the end that the shooting was an accident carried out when he was drunk.

Alfred Bowker from Winchester had his own ideas about what should be done to prevent such outrages in future. He wrote to *The Times* with his ideas. He was particularly concerned because he had travelled on the same train as Pearson. The fact that the compartments were partitioned from each other isolated passengers from one another. Therefore:

> we might at least take a leaf from our Continental friends, for in France and many other places we almost invariably find, when their railway coaches are divided by partitions into several compartments, each compartment has a means of communication by a sliding glass panel, which is inserted in the partitions slightly above the heads of passengers when seated.

People could then speak to others in other compartments and also see what was happening there. This would deter crime, because people in another compartment could see what was happening and then ring the communication cord. It would also reassure nervous passengers. It does not seem that this suggestion found favour.

This murder was hardly original. As with Muller in 1864 and Mapleton in 1881, Parker was a desperate young man in need of money. Selecting as his victim, a prosperous-looking man, he killed him for his money, but was subsequently arrested, tried and hanged; just as his predecessors had been. However, unlike them, he had accelerated the progress of his discovery and arrest by committing his crime in the presence of another, and this was a fatal error. Had he been even more ruthless than he was, he could have shot her dead as well, and this would certainly have delayed his apprehension; whether he would have escaped justice as other train killers in the future were to do is a moot point. Perhaps he would have done.

7

The Mystery of Merstham Tunnel, 1905

'I can't let you have it, I am going to meet a particular "Tart" tomorrow.'

On Sunday evening of 24 September 1905, the body of a young woman was found on the railway line in Merstham tunnel. At first it seemed that this was either a case of accident or suicide. The body was conveyed to the stables of the nearby Feathers Hotel. PC Burt and PC Carr were the first two policemen on the scene. On closer examination it appeared that this was a case of murder. This was because a scarf was found in her mouth; it was about ten inches within, though fairly loose, but was difficult to pull out. Furthermore, both her purse and her ticket were missing. Superintendent Brice of Surrey Police was in charge of the investigation.

Most of the public facts of the case were disclosed at the two hearings of the inquest, both held at the coffee room of the Feathers Hotel. The inquest was concluded on 2 October. Mr Nightingale, coroner of East Surrey, presided and Brice and Captain Sant of the Surrey Constabulary were also present.

The first fact to emerge was the identity of the victim. She was Miss Mary Sophia Money, born in 1882 in Watford. In 1901 she was employed as a book-keeper in a dairy and then lived in Harrow Wealdstone. By 1905, she was the book-keeper at Henry Bridger's dairy on Lavender Hill, Battersea. The dairy was actually managed by his brother, Arthur, who did not, unlike the rest of his staff, sleep on the premises. Her wage was 8s per week, plus board and lodging. She had taken the place of Miss Lane, who had been employed there for four years, but who had to leave to look after her sick sister. Her savings amounted to £50 on death. Miss Money's wages were raised from 6s to 8s a week before her death, because the nature of her duties changed. She was apparently a good worker and the accounts were in order.

Her injuries were horrific. The top of the head and forehead were broken, with the brains being partially torn and out and smashed. Her nose bones were broken. There were other fractures to the skull. Only the lower part of the face was unaffected. There were also bruises around her mouth and on the rest of her body, together with a number of scratches.

Many of these injuries could have been, and undoubtedly were, the result of leaving the train suddenly and then been run over by it. However, there were some which had probably not been inflicted in that way. Dr Wilcox stated:

> There were several bruises on the left arm of a livid colour – deep crimson. One ran along the forearm. It was so red that it looked as if it had been stamped on. There were also other bruises above the elbow. On the left hand I found a small crimson bruise on the back of the little finger, this being the only mark on the left hand. On the upper extremity of the right arm I found several dark crimson bruises very clearly defined. Over the front of the bend of the right elbow was a pale blue bruise of a different colour. Another light blue bruise was also found.

The coroner pressed the doctor for his conclusions. He replied, 'I think they were produced in quite a different way from the others. The others were the result of very considerable violence.' He thought that she had been alive on leaving the train, and that the bruises on the arm and hand were produced by someone's grip. They might have been caused by a struggle. If she was defending herself, then it was probable that she would have used her right arm in order to do so (Miss Money was right-handed according to her brother). Some of the other bruises might have been caused by her body being thrust through the compartment door or window.

Emma Hone, a colleague of the victim, gave her evidence. She had helped Miss Money to dress on the evening of 24 September. She had worn a wide white silk scarf around her neck. Although Miss Money had told her she would be back by 9 pm, she had not returned home that night by 11 pm. Their employer, Mr Bridger, came down from the dining room and asked Miss Hone if she could wait up for Miss Money. She agreed and went up to her colleague's room. Although her latchkey was in her bag in the room, she herself was not there. Miss Hone waited there for two hours, but to no avail. At 1 am she went to bed.

Relatively little was known about Miss Money's last movements. In the afternoon, she had been studying railway timetables, according to a colleague. A railway journey was evidently being planned, and one that was not simple. Her planned route, though, was kept secret. She spoke with her manager that morning. Early in the evening she had gone to Miss Frances Golding's shop near Clapham Junction. Here she bought a box of chocolates after being in the shop for about 5–7 minutes. She was alone. It was then about 7 pm and she told Miss Golding that she was going to Victoria (a very short trip from Clapham Junction). She was next seen at Clapham Junction station. Here, though, the evidence varies. Edward Parker, a ticket collector at the station, said that when the 7.21 train left that evening, he saw a young woman, whom he later identified as Miss Money, standing on the platform. He asked her where she was going and she said Victoria. She was alone. However, David Morris, a tailor of Hampton, said he saw a young woman, whom he believed was Miss Money, at Victoria at about 7.20 pm. He had been waiting there for the arrival of his son. When shown a photograph of her, he thought that the woman he saw was very similar. Clearly both witnesses could not be correct, but as to which was correct was impossible to discern.

Another witness claimed they saw her at Victoria. Mrs Macilroy, a schoolmistress at a boarding school, recalled that, at 7.30 pm, at Victoria:

> I saw a lady enter the station from Wilton Road, and from what I read, I am now convinced that this lady was Miss Money. She appeared to be expecting somebody and although she kept walking up and down, I noticed that she was always looking towards the Buckingham Palace entrance. About 7.45, as she was being rather annoyed by gentlemen looking at her, she was joined by a gentleman, carrying a brown kit bag and wearing a pepper and salt coloured coat, who apparently came into the station from the Buckingham Palace entrance. The greeting struck me as very unusual. The gentleman did not sit down, and both went off together immediately, towards the other station.

It was then thought that she was seen at Croydon station. Alfred

Barton, a guard on the London, Brighton and South Coast Railway, was on the 9.13 train from London Bridge on the night in question. He was talking to a man on the platform at Croydon just in front of a first class carriage, no. 508. He then saw a man and a woman walking past the barrier. The woman was young and wore dark clothes, with a long muslin scarf. She was tall and thin and her companion was thin, five feet eight high and had a long face and a thin chin. The man was wearing a bowler hat and had a moustache. He saw the couple again at the next station, South Croydon. They were sitting very close together in a compartment. The man sat on the side nearest the door.

When questioned more closely, Barton gave additional details. He thought the pair were behaving suspiciously by trying to avoid him. He wondered if they were in fact, first class passengers. Barton said, 'When I looked at the man in South Croydon he looked as if he didn't want anything to do with me.' The next stop was Redhill, where the guard, though he was occupied with the mail van, thought that the man alighted. Earlier, he had merely said that he had not actually seen the man leave, but that he had seen a porter shutting the door. Whether or not he had indeed seen Miss Money and her companion is another question. The two may well have been merely eager to avoid the guard because they were having an illicit affair, rather than anything more deadly.

There was an interesting statement by Frederick Yarnley, a signalman on duty at Purley Oaks signal box. He saw the train which had left London Bridge at 9.13 pass by. He also saw a struggle take place in one of the compartments on that same train, in the carriage which was third from the end of the train. A couple was apparently standing up, and the man was trying to force the woman onto the seat. The man had both his hands up and the struggle took place near to the door, not the communication cord. The woman was about five feet four and was dressed in black. He did not notice whether she was wearing a scarf. He could not identify the woman he had seen with a photograph of Miss Money. Such sights, though uncommon, were not rare and it did not, in his opinion, seem to be of sufficient severity that would justify in stopping the train.

A possible clue was a handkerchief found at Penge. Robert Money was uncertain whether his sister's handkerchiefs were marked, but thought they had lace around the edges.

It certainly seems that Miss Money was seeing a man. An anonymous man said he saw her on the Sunday before her death, involved in 'a heated alteration in the neighbourhood of Clapham station'. It was reported by another informant that Miss Money often went to the Crichton restaurant, near to Clapham Junction, with a well-dressed man. They were seen there on the Wednesday and Friday afternoons before her death, and allegedly the same man accompanied her to the station on the Sunday evening.

One suspect who would seem to have been ruled out was Charles Bell, a railway clerk. He had known Miss Money for four years, though there had been no engagement nor any understanding between them. However, he had given her a ring in the previous year. He had last seen her on 18 September. On the day of her death he was on a cycling trip with a friend, Mr Morris. They had had tea at The George at Berkhamsted in west Hertfordshire, and had not returned to London until 9 pm. He knew of no other man that she was seeing.

Another suspect was Bridger himself. There was some discussion whether his relationship with Miss Money might be more than merely that of employer and employee. George Money claimed that Bridger had once been with her to Waterloo station, where she took a cab to Euston. She did not tell him if Bridger paid for it. When asked about Bridger, Miss Money told her brother that 'he was a very nice fellow'. She was apparently cheerful in her life and work. Money told the court that his sister said that Bridger told her that he made about £6 per week. On a Sunday in the previous summer, according to her sister, Miss Money went down to Bognor with Bridger and when the latter saw a man from Clapham, who worked at a furniture shop near to the dairy, he turned his face away in order not to be recognized. Once she had been to the theatre with Bridger and her brother. It was also alleged that on 17 September, Bridger went with her to Clapham Junction, where she took a train to Windsor (buying a second class ticket) and it was expected he would meet her on her return. The two clearly appeared to spend time together outside working hours. Finally, Money claimed he saw Bridger after the murder with injured fingers.

Both Bridger and Caroline, his wife, vehemently denied this. He said he had never given her any gift, nor had he discussed his income with her, nor did he ever go to the theatre with her. Although he had been at the dairy shop on the Sunday, he had left at 2.30 to go home, where he dined with his wife. He then smoked and lay on his bed until about 7 pm. Then the couple had tea and went out for a stroll on the Common before retiring to bed at about 10.30. They were childless and did not employ a servant on Sundays. No one was able to corroborate the story, but there was no direct evidence against him, nor did anyone see him with Miss Money on that fatal night. The clean-shaven Bridger was asked by a juror if he wore a moustache, which he denied.

Captain Sant was interested in the possibility that Bridger was responsible and encouraged his men to investigate this. He wrote, 'I should be very much obliged if you could kindly take steps to find whether there is anything in these statements.' However, after it seemed that Bridger was not with Miss Money that evening, Sant came to another conclusion, and noted that 'Deceased told lies about not only Arthur Bridger but other persons'. We don't know exactly what information was uncovered by the police here, but it was presumably convincing.

James Brosh, of the engineers' department of the South Eastern and Chatham railway, produced a map of the tunnel. His examination of the place had found a mark along the roof which stopped abruptly 35 feet after the point where the corpse had been found. It was very regular and had to have been made by something hard and sharp. It could have been made by someone holding a stick, but it would have had to have been a powerful man to have held a stick so. It might, of course, have been made after the death. Whether it had any relevance was another question.

Inspector Warren of the railway company police discussed his findings. He had travelled in carriage 508 on a 9.13 from London Bridge. The total width of a carriage door was 27 inches and that exceeded the space between the train and the tunnel wall. The door could only have been opened about eight inches if opened in the tunnel. When asked by the coroner if a body could have got out in the tunnel, he answered, 'I think it would have been impossible.' However, a juror claimed that he could have got through a gap of eight inches. The coroner noted that no signs of blood had been found on the carriage door.

Superintendent Brice gave the jury the results of the initial police investigations. Every clue had been followed up, but all had led to dead ends. Over a hundred people, including railway employees, had been questioned by the Surrey Police and by Scotland Yard detectives. But after Miss Money's leaving the sweet shop, nothing could be ascertained of her movements.

The coroner was undecided what the verdict should be before the jury came up with their conclusion. It took them 70 minutes before they could do so. When they did, the foreman said:

> The jury are unanimously of opinion that the deceased met her death through injuries brought about by a train, but the evidence is insufficient to show whether she was thrown from a train or fell from a train accidentally.

The jury passed their sympathy to Miss Money's family. The coroner then stated, 'Your verdict is practically an open verdict. You do not think the evidence sufficient to justify you in coming to any more definite conclusion?' The foreman replied:

> That is so. We understand that the police are anxious to pursue the enquiries further, and it was the greatest wish of the jury to give a verdict which would not hamper the police in any way. If it lay in their power they would render all the help they could.

Not everyone thought it was murder. Chief Inspector Fox was convinced that this was a case of suicide, but if so why did Miss Money dress up for the occasion, and why was there no note? Furthermore, nobody seemed to think she was in low spirits.

On the same day that the inquest was completed, the body was taken to Merstham station and then put on a train to Watford. There were six wreaths on the coffin and Robert Money, her brother, accompanied it.

There were a number of suggestions later made to the police. Henry White, from Shadwell, was alleged by an anonymous source to be the killer. But, on investigation, no one of that name was known there. Another writer suggested that a platform porter at Clapham Junction was the killer. This man was called 'Rose'. He was aged 31, of medium build, had a moustache and was of good appearance. He was married and lived with his wife at St John's Hill Grove in Wandsworth. He was reputed to be having an affair with a young woman and he was often home late at night, after travelling on the railways. He was also well dressed and well off. This lead was either not followed up or was rejected.

An anonymous letter also gave further information about Miss Money. Apparently in 1902 she had had a dairy business at

Marlborough Road in Harrow Wealdstone. Because of faulty produce, she was fined £6. Yet this seemed an unlikely story because she would have only been 18 at the time, which seems very young for a woman to be in business.

Police investigations continued for some years. There were a number of suggested leads, but none led anywhere. For instance, in 1906, the activities of Josiah Smith, alias Fred Mcleod, were unmasked, and he received nine months in gaol. He was a confidence trickster who duped unsuspecting women out of their savings. There was press speculation that he might have been involved with Miss Money, but since murder was not part of his repertoire, it seems hard not to agree with the police comment on the theory, 'All this originated from the imagination of a reporter.'

A more promising lead, perhaps, came from Albert Cooper, a stable help and motor car cleaner, who had resided in a room in Lansdown House in 1904–8. He thought that a fellow resident, William Wakeman, a liftman, might have been the killer. There were several connections between him and the victim. He said that Wakeman had gone to school with Miss Money in Watford and often went to Lavendear Hill where she lived and worked, but never visited the district thereafter. Wakeman had also been a coachman employed by Crosse & Blackwell near Harrow and Miss Money had once lived in Harrow. On the Saturday just before the murder, Cooper had asked Wakeman if he could borrow his walking stick. Cooper replied, 'I can't let you have it, I am going to meet a particular "Tart" tomorrow'. Cooper explained to Inspector Arthur Hailstone that he had not contacted the police hitherto because he felt he could not trust anyone. However, the police conclusion was that they 'Can find no direct evidence upon which anyone could be charged.'

There were a couple of other suggestions. Charles Johnson, who was in Edinburgh prison in 1909 confessed to the murder. Yet it was found that he was in York gaol at the time of the killing, so was ruled out. In the same year, James Raven, a convict in Brixton prison, said that he had relevant information, but would only part with it if he were paid. He was in gaol on the charge of begging and the theft of a gold watch. Any information he had was deemed to be useless.

All that is certain is that Miss Money left her place of employment on Sunday 24 September 1905 and went to buy chocolates in a sweet shop near Clapham Junction. She then almost certainly took a train from that busy station. The train was one which stopped at East Croydon, where she changed for the 9.13 from London Bridge. Again, it seems fairly certain that at some point that evening she met a man, probably by prior appointment (hence the concern about her appearance before she went out). Who that man was is unknown, but he was clearly her killer. He may have assaulted her before going into the tunnel and there pushed her out of the carriage and onto the line, gagging her first so she could not cry out. He then alighted at the next station and went on his way. Why he killed her is unclear. It does not seem that robbery or rape were motives. Perhaps he wanted to end the affair, perhaps he was being blackmailed, perhaps the man was married and could not afford the scandal. Bridger would seem to be a possible suspect, having been married and having recently raised her salary (blackmail?), but we must be careful. Although he did not have a strong alibi – loved ones have been known to provide killers with alibis – no one saw the two together and there is no direct evidence implicating him, or anyone else. The mystery is as cloudy now as it was in 1905.

A grim footnote to the case is that in 1912 Robert Money killed the two women he had been simultaneously having affairs with, before shooting himself. Indeed, the Money family was a most unfortunate one.

8

The Newcastle to Alnmouth Railway Murder, 1910

'It is absurd for me to deny the charge, because it is absurd to make it, but I absolutely deny it.'

On 4 July 1910 at Northumberland Assizes, John Alexander Dickman, stood accused of murder. He was aged 45, was married and with at least two children. In 1910, the family lived at Lily Avenue, Jesmond, Newcastle. The family's finances, though, were in a parlous state and Dickman had been borrowing money where he could. Mrs Annie Dickman, a former teacher, had two savings accounts; one with the Newcastle savings bank. In January 1910, the sums in these were £15 9d and £17 11d; but in March the latter account only had £4 in it and on the day before the murder, this was reduced to £2. There is no doubt that penury seemed imminent, and it should also be noted that Dickman was not in paid employment at this time; nor had he been since 1906, when he had been a secretary at a colliery at Morpeth. He was a gambler and ran up many debts. He had asked William Hogg, a former employer, for loans on several occasions in 1910. Just before the murder, Mrs Dickman had told her husband, 'With my dividend due this week and what is in the post office, I dare say it will pay the most pressing things, but it is going to make the question of living a poser unless you can give me some advice as to what to do.' Pressing demands included a last demand for rates and money for their son's schooling.

We now need to return to the events of what had been a fatal day, 18 March. John Innes Nisbet, a 44-year-old married man, who lived at Heaton Road, Newcastle, was employed as a clerk and book-keeper by the Stobswood Colliery, Widdrington. On every alternate Friday, he had to collect the money to pay the workers. This was brought from Lloyds' Bank in Newcastle. Friday 18 March was one such day. He went to the bank with a cheque from the company made payable to cash. Then the money, a total of £371 9s 6d, was made out in silver and gold and put into a bag.

He then took the cash and went to Newcastle Central Railway Station, to take a North Eastern Company train to Alnmouth. Charles Raven thought he saw Nisbet and Dickman walking together. Dickman was certainly not alone on the station platform, but Wilson Hepple, an artist who knew him, could not identify his companion. Percival Harding Hall, a clerk, saw two men, one of whom was Nisbet, board the 10.27 train from platform 5. He got into a third class compartment in the first carriage of the train behind the engine.

The train consisted of the engine and four carriages. The first one consisted of third class compartments and a luggage compartment. The second was composed of a first class compartment sandwiched between two third class ones. The third carriage was of third class accommodation only. The final one was a mixture of third class and luggage compartments.

The second stop was Heaton. Here Cicely Elizabeth Nisbet spoke to her husband, as she customarily did. She saw another man in the same compartment, but he was sitting in the shadows and she could only make out his profile. She later said, 'when speaking to my husband at Heaton station, the view in profile I got of my husband's companion did not enable me to identify him as anyone who I knew'. She only knew Dickman by sight. Nisbet was still alive when the train left the Stannington station, the next stop, at 11.06. Hall alighted there and saw him, and nodded to him. John William Spink, a clerk and his companion, confirmed seeing him there. There was still another man with Nisbet, but he could not be identified. However, at the next station, Morpeth, a witness stated, after a cursory look, that no one seemed to be in the compartment which Nisbet had entered.

It was not until the train reached its final destination, Alnmouth, at 12.06, 23 miles from Newcastle, that a shocking discovery was made by Thomas Charlton. Underneath the seat was the dead body of Nisbet. There were four bullets in his head. Two were nickel coated and two were lead revolver cartridges. Two were small and two were large. Three of these bullets were twisted out of shape. There was also paper wadding found there. Although it was thought that two revolvers had been used in the murder, it was probably only one; paper wadding could have been inserted into the chambers where two small bullets were loaded in each. Of the money bag, there was, of course, no sign. It was thought that he must have been killed between Stannington and Morpeth. And one of the passengers who alighted from the train at Morpeth was Dickman, a fact he later readily admitted.

Three days after the murder, following a lead from Raven, Detective Inspector Tait paid a visit to Dickman's home. He accompanied them to the central police station and made a voluntary statement about his movements on that day. However, curiously enough for a man up to his neck in debt, the not inconsiderable sum of £17 9s 11d was found on his person. For a clerk, this was about two months' wages.

Dickman, then, gave his own account of what he had done that day.

> I knew Nisbet for many years. I saw him that morning. I booked at the ticket office after him, and went by the same train, but I didn't see him after the train left. On Friday morning last I went to the central station and took a return ticket for Stannington. Nisbet, the deceased man, whom I knew, was at the ticket office before me, and so far as I know, had left the hall by the time I had got mine. I went to the bookstall and got a newspaper, The Manchester Sporting Chronicle. I then went to the refreshment room and had a pie and a pint of ale. I then went on the platform and took my seat in a third class carriage nearer the hinder end of the train than the front end. My recollection is, though I am not quite clear on the matter, that people entered and left the compartment at different stations on the journey. The train passed Stannington station without my noticing it, and I got out at Morpeth, and handed my ticket, and the excess fare of 2 1/2d to the collector. I left Morpeth to walk to Stannington by the main road. I took ill of diarrheoa on the way, and had to return to Morpeth to catch the 1.12 train, but I missed it and I got the 1.40 at Morpeth. After missing the 1.12 train, I came out of the station on the east side and turned down towards the town. I met a man named Elliott and spoke to him. I did not get into the town but turned and went back to the station, and got the 1.40 slow train to Newcastle. I got a single ticket for Stannington and did not give it up.

Apparently he made the journey because he wanted to see a William Hogg of Dovecote, near Stannington, about a new sinking operation that was to take place there soon. No appointment was made and Hogg did not see Dickman. Hogg had previously lent Dickman money. John Athley the ticket collector at Morpeth remembered taking an excess fare there and that the man who he dealt with resembled Dickman, but he could not be absolutely certain it was him.

There were also physical clues. On 9 June, the money bag was found at the bottom of a mine shaft by Robert Spooner, a colliery manager, at Hepscott. This was a mile and a half from Morpeth. Dickman's clothes were also examined. Bloodstains were found on his gloves and these had made marks in his trouser pockets. Dr Bolam, professor at Durham University College of Medicine, examined all these, and also Dickman's overcoat. There was a smear of blood on the thumb on the left-hand glove. There were also recent stains on the trouser pocket, but it could not be ascertained what these were. There were also paraffin stains on his coat and these could have been the result of attempts to clear other substances from the coat. Dickman explained these away by saying he often had nose bleeds and the paraffin stains were the result of bicycle oil.

A Newcastle newsagent recalled, in January 1910, that a parcel containing a revolver was handed in at her shop. It was addressed to Dickman, and had, she believed, been subsequently collected by him. This may have been the automatic magazine pistol which he had bought in 1907 from W H Pape & Co., gunsmiths of Newcastle. The nickel coated bullets could have been fired by one of this type of gun. Of course, such guns and ammunition could be purchased in any gunsmith's shop.

Some witnesses picked out Dickman from an identity parade. Hall was one and Spink was another. Yet doubt must be cast upon the veracity of their evidence. Apparently a policeman suggested that the two should look at Dickman as he was then being examined. They saw the back of his head and his coat. Hall said that this did not influence him in picking out Dickman from an identity parade. Dickman was wearing a light-coloured coat, and one of this colour had been worn by the man seen with Nisbet. There had also been conversation between detectives and the witnesses beforehand, though it did not, apparently, concern the identification of Dickman. Even so, this was all very irregular and reprehensible.

When Mrs Nisbet saw Dickman in the magistrates' court, he was in the same position and the same profile as the man who had been in the same compartment as her husband on that fatal Friday. Such was her emotion, she fainted.

The police certainly thought that the case against Dickman was a strong one. Dickman was arrested and on 15 April, he was brought before Newcastle magistrates' court. His defence stressed that, although there was much suspicion and suggestion against Dickman, there was a lack of hard evidence. All the witnesses had failed to state definitely that Dickman and Nisbet were together in the same compartment. It was demanded that Dickman be set free. A plea of not guilty was registered. After the magistrates left the court for half an hour, the chairman told the court that a case had been made against the accused and he would then be remanded until the Assizes in the summer. Dickman all along utterly refuted the charges against him. On one occasion he said, 'I don't understand the proceedings. It is absurd for me to deny the charge, because it is absurd to make it, but I absolutely deny it.'

The actual trial began on 4 July at the Northumberland Assizes held at the Moot Hall, Newcastle, before Justice Coleridge. Mr Tindal Atkinson KC and Mr Lowenthal prosecuted and Dickman was defended by Mr Michael-Innes KC and Lord William Percy made the case for the accused. Atkinson admitted at the outset that the case rested entirely on circumstantial evidence. The evidence against Dickman has already been stated. Dickman gave evidence on behalf of himself, a relatively new procedure – first seen in the case of Robert Wood in 1907. On that earlier occasion, it worked in the accused's favour (the case is told in the author's *Unsolved Murders in Victorian and Edwardian London*). The judge summed up on 6 July. Dickman was found guilty and sentenced to death. Perhaps it is worth noting that the jury took almost three hours to deliver their verdict. It had not been an easy decision to make.

Yet, thanks to another new legal innovation (the Criminal Appeal Act of 1907), anyone condemned to death could have their case referred to the Court of Criminal Appeal. This was the case here. It was heard on 22 July before the Lord Chief Justice and Mr Justice Phillmore. The same men appeared for prosecution and defence. Mr Mitchell-Innes, speaking for Dickman, said that Dickman's wife had not been allowed to speak in his defence, that the judge had misdirected the jury and that some of the evidence had been withdrawn before the jury. His main argument was that the identity of the man with Nisbet could not be proved to have been Dickman and that the witness statements had been inconclusive. Attention was particularly drawn to the fact that there may have been an attempt made by the police to point out Dickman to the witnesses before trying to pick him out of an identity parade. It was not enough to prove motive; opportunity was also required, and for this, it had to be shown that Dickman and Nisbet had travelled together the same compartment on the train. He alleged that the prosecution had been unable to do so. The Lord Chief Justice admitted that any attempt by the police to undermine the independence of identity by witnesses was reprehensible, but he did not think that this wholly undermined the case against Dickman, and that circumstantial evidence in this case was strong enough to be conclusive. The appeal was quashed.

Shortly afterwards, there was a petition for clemency forwarded to Winston Churchill, the Home Secretary, by Edward Clark. It received the following response:

> I am directed by the Home Secretary to inform you that he has given careful consideration to the petition submitted by you on behalf of John Alexander Dickman, now under sentence of death . . . and I have to express to you his regret that, after considering all the circumstances of the case, he has failed to discover any grounds which will justify him in advising His Majesty to interfere with the due course of the law.

A few days later, while a batch of signatures were again despatched for a reprieve, a woman made a signed statement to Mr Clark to this effect. She had been in Leazes Park, Newcastle, on the day after Dickman's arrest and heard two men discussing the disposal of a body under a railway seat. They then became quiet when they realized she could hear them. On being asked by them what she had heard, she replied in the negative for fear of what they might otherwise do to her. She eventually came forward, despite her fear that they might be following her, because it was on her conscience and she could not sleep.

Although many in Newcastle sympathised with Dickman, many did not. On one trip to see her husband in prison, Mrs Dickman was booed by a crowd outside the gaol, and letters in the local press hotly contested the issue. One wrote, 'Dickman convicted! Who then is safe? No actual proof. Suspicion, if you like. He should have had the benefit of the doubt. The evidence was not strong enough to hang a dog on.' Another wrote, 'I venture to say that 9 persons out of every 10 are of the opinion that Dickman has been found guilty on evidence which, besides being circumstantial, is woefully inadequate.' But other people thought that the verdict was safe, and one wrote:

> As another earnest student of the train murder, I, with the majority of others, consider the verdict passed on Dickman a very proper and fit one, and too good for such an undoubted scoundrel. Evidently we have a lot of unbalanced morbid sentimentalists amongst us. Anyone with a grain of commonsense would certainly agree that no other verdict was possible.

Dickman never ceased to pronounce his own innocence. On the day before he died, he wrote a letter to his wife, which included the following sentences, 'There is something still keeps telling me that everything will be made clear some day, when it is too late to benefit me. I can only repeat that I am innocent.' Yet the course of the law was relentless. On 10 August, Dickman was executed, an inquest on his body discovering that death was instantaneous. When he was executed, about 1,500 people had gathered outside the prison. As a local newspaper observed, 'Interest in the crime for which Dickman paid the extreme penalty of the law was maintained to the last.'

The other side of the coin was that Mrs Nisbet applied under the Workmen's Compensation Act, for any money the company might give her on behalf of her husband being killed under their employ. The Act was designed to compensate employees and their families for the loss of life and limb in factory or industrial accidents. The employers denied that Nisbet's murder fell within this remit, but Mrs Nisbet's case went her way because it was said that her husband had died whilst at work; he would not have been killed if he had not been carrying the firm's wages. She was awarded £300. She also benefited by £302 11s 2d from her husband's will.

Train design was also commented on by a local newspaper:

> Thanks to the antiquated system which divides British railway coaches into a series of rigidly separated cells, there have been previous tragedies of a not dissimilar kind, but the menaces to public safety which lies in the possibility of such a crime being committed at almost any time, when the motive is sufficiently

strong was never more clearly brought forward than in this instance.

Yet, as in earlier cases, this type of remark went unheeded. Perhaps the desire for privacy overcame concerns for security.

There was controversy over the verdict in this murder case both at the time and subsequently. Modern science would have been able to clarify it, by the use of testing of the substances on Dickman's clothes. However, without such tests, we are in the realm of supposition. The killer was almost certainly someone who knew Nisbet and who was at Newcastle station in time to catch the 10.27 on 18 March 1910. He probably alighted at Morpeth. He had a revolver and was motivated by financial gain. He clearly was intent on murder and had planned his crime ahead of his travels that day. All this would fit in with Dickman. But, of course, there may well have been other men who fit this profile. Although Dickman's guilt seems highly probable, it is not entirely proven beyond reasonable doubt. A recent study of the murder, however, concludes that it was planned out in advance and the stolen money well hidden by the killer – Dickman.

9

Murder on the Brighton Line, 1914

'If any of you had been treated in the same way you would
have done the same.'

It was Saturday night of 25 April 1914. Liverpool and Burnley had just
played in the FA Cup Final at Crystal Palace (Burnley won, one goal to
nil, with George V awarding the cup to the winning team). The train on
the London Brighton and South Coast Railway had left London Bridge
at 7.20 pm. It was scheduled to arrive at Brighton at 9.10 and its first stop
was East Croydon. Thereafter, it was a stopping service at every station
between there and its destination. At Horley station, two lovers boarded
a third class compartment, and were apparently lively and were joking
with each other, claimed a witness. They intended to travel to Horley, but
bought tickets that would take them to the next station, which was Three
Bridges, only a mile and a half away. The two had been drinking earlier
that day, then had had tea in a restaurant. It is time we were introduced
to them, but their short-lived journey was far from romantic.

The man was Herbert Brooker, aged 32. He was born in Hove, Sussex,
on 8 April 1882, and had joined the Royal Navy on 8 April 1900, after
having worked as an errand boy. Brooker was five feet five inches tall,
with grey eyes, a fresh complexion and had a scald mark on his face. He
had served for twelve years, including spells on board thirteen ships, such
as HMS *Powerful*, *Cressy*, *Wellington*, *Hindustan* and the *Excellent*. He left
on 11 April 1912 as a leading seaman gunner with an excellent character
and joined the Royal Naval Reserve. He had then served in other vessels,
including the *Lusitania* (controversially sunk in 1915 by a German
submarine) and various ocean-going tramps. More recently he had been
working on shore, and by about March 1914 had been given a permanent
post at the Port of London Authority, where he had been working on a
temporary contract since August 1913. Things certainly seemed to be
looking up for him. He was a well-known figure in Horley, because he

lodged there with his brother-in-law at Mrs Mate's, whenever he was around. He had told people there that his companion would soon be coming down to Crawley and that the two of them had had their banns already published, so marriage was imminent.

His companion, and apparently soon to be wife, was Mrs Ada Stone. She was 29 and was five feet six in height, with brown hair and a sallow complexion. That day she was wearing a blue skirt and jacket, with a white blouse and a blue hat. There was a ring on the third finger of her right hand. Yet there was a difficulty in the way of Brooker's marital intentions. On 15 February 1909 she had been married to a man who had left her at least by 1911, but she was, of course, still legally married. Oddly enough, the census entry of 1911 states she was a widow. Her husband had not been heard of for some time. The problem was to be resolved by Brooker by putting an advert in a newspaper for the missing man. She had once been the manageress at a Woolwich restaurant and then worked as a cook at the Royal Albert Docks there. In 1914 she was employed by Mrs Fitches in Woolwich High Street.

She lived on the premises, but had last slept there on 19 April. On the following evening, she went to bed at 9. Brooker called for her then, rather worse for drink. Mrs Fitches woke up Mrs Stone, and the latter went with Brooker. She returned on 21 April and argued with Mrs Fitches. She then left and was last seen in a tramcar.

Their journey on 25 April 1914 did not go as planned. Between a mile and half a mile from Three Bridges station, the communication cord was pulled. Not by either Brooker or his companion – it was rung three times by a young man who was two compartments away. This was Donald Palmer of Woodford Green. He heard a sound like a child's cry, then a loud laugh and then a shriek. He looked through the window and saw a woman on the floor, with a man with a knife standing over her. However, the train's guard, Albert Hillman, although he told the driver about this, he did not suggest that the train be stopped. He thought it would be safer if the train proceeded to Three Bridges and the matter, whatever it was, could be dealt with there.

When the train arrived at Three Bridges station, Brooker stepped down from the compartment. He was described as being a well-set young man. He had a sailor's knife in his hand. Hillman and Inspector Robbins, with other staff and passengers, apprehended him and took the knife from his hand. They found some rope and bound him, before taking him to the waiting room. The police were called and Superintendent Budgen of Crawley and two constables drove to the scene of the crime. Brooker asked 'Is she dead?' When Budgen asked him who he was, he replied, 'I do not think I can tell you.'

Brooker was given some water and the ropes were removed. He appeared very agitated. He was found to have a small bottle of whisky on him, which was removed. Brooker said to Robbins, 'You ought to have a Victoria Cross' and then said, 'Let me get at him', but it is unclear to whom this referred. He also appeared fatalistic about his own fate:

> I hope I shall be strung up. I deserve it. She was a good girl. I did what I wanted, and am satisfied. It was a mad frenzy. If any of you had been treated in the same way you would have done the same.

Meanwhile, Ronald Mackay, a local chauffeur, who had been waiting on the platform for his mother, stepped into the compartment from which Brooker had just alighted. He made a shocking discovery. There he saw a young woman lying dead. Her throat had been cut. Although he did not know who it was, this was the body of Mrs Stone.

The corpse was taken to the stationmaster's office. Here it was examined by Dr Matthews of Crawley. He found there were two deep wounds in the chest and one in her back. Both she and Brooker were wearing Burnley colours – they had been to the football match.

Mrs Stone's body was identified that night by her sister, Mrs Maud Newstead, also of Woolwich, who came down with her husband to perform this unpleasant duty. She had not seen her sister since Easter.

What had happened in that third class compartment? Mrs Mackay gave her account:

> I was alone. When the train stopped at Horley I saw Brooker and a young woman looking into the carriage windows. When the train was approaching Three Bridges, I heard a bell ringing constantly, but no screaming. As the train drew into the station, I put my head out of the window and saw Brooker jump out of the next compartment with a large knife in his hand.

Apparently Brooker shouted 'I want my Ada. I want my Ada. I admit I've done it.'

The inquest was held on 27 April at East Grinstead. Brooker was charged with murder. He was asked no further questions, but was remanded in custody for another week, being placed in Lewes gaol. At the adjourned inquest, Hillman was a leading witness. This was because of the controversy over him not having the train stopped when the cord was pulled. He said that when he first heard it, he looked out of the window to see if he could see anything amiss. The train was then passing by the signal box at Tinsley Green. Nothing seemed to be wrong. He explained his inaction thus, 'I used my discretion and it was in the exercise of that discretion that I intended to run on to the Three Bridges station'. He gave the driver the white light to proceed, as opposed to telling the driver to shut off the steam and so stop the train. He explained it would be easier and safer to find out the source of the problem at a station than in between them. The jury agreed that Hillman acted correctly. They also commended Palmer for pulling the cord. The inquest concluded that Mrs Stone had been murdered and that Brooker was the killer.

The trial took place at the Sussex Assizes on 7 July, before Justice Daly. Although there was no doubt that Brooker had killed Mrs Stone, the defence did their best. They said that Brooker was drunk and so he could only be charged with the lesser crime of manslaughter, not murder. They stressed his excellent character as seen by his naval service. The reason he carried a knife was not due to any evil intention towards Mrs Stone, but because he had been attacked by a gang of men whilst on his way to work and so, presumably, needed it for self-defence. However, the jury thought otherwise and Brooker was sentenced to death.

It is unclear why Brooker killed Mrs Stone. The two appeared to be fond of one another, and there was no prior evidence of any violence between them. Even when Brooker was in drink, he had not been known to hit her. Brooker said himself:

> We had been drinking and dancing and were pretty well oiled up when something cropped up and I did it. If I had done it half an hour later they would not have collared me. At least, not so fast. I had been carrying the knife down my leg for the past fortnight, but I shifted it the same day that it happened to my waist.

Presumably the two must have had some form of drunken quarrel almost immediately after boarding the train. What it concerned, we don't know. Presumably no third party was involved or was imagined to be.

Brooker was executed at Lewes prison on 28 July 1914 by John Ellis and Thomas Pierrepoint.

10

The Most Foul of Murders, 1915

'It was the biggest manhunt in the City of London'

Perhaps the worst of all the crimes in this book is the one to be described in this chapter. Child murder was not unknown at the time, and there was the case of Willie Strachfield killed on the Underground in the year previous to this one (outlined in Chapter 21 below). But this one was even worse.

On Saturday 3 April 1915, Margaret Ellen Nally celebrated her seventh and last birthday. She lived with her family on Amberley Road, Harrow Road, Paddington. Her father, John Henry Nally, was a night porter at Paddington. She attended All Angels' School at Cirencester Street. She had two brothers, one aged 9, the other aged 4, and a 13-month-old sister.

The following day was Easter Day. At 3.30 pm, Margaret went to see her aunt and other family members. They lived on Carlisle Road, Edgware. It was about half an hour's walk, but no one seems to have had any apprehension of her travelling alone there. She had made the trip before and was always back before dark. Moreover, she knew the neighbourhood well, was intelligent and didn't speak to strangers. No one had ever offered her sweets nor had accosted her previously. And there was certainly no problem with her trip there. She arrived at her aunt's, Mrs Betsy Scott. There she played with her 5-year-old cousin, Alice Scott, as well as seeing her aunt and grandfather.

The two little girls ran an errand for Margaret's aunt, going to buy her some matches from Emily Knight's shop, and she rewarded them with a penny each. They bought some sweets at a shop in the street, perhaps one run by a Mrs Walker, and then said their goodbyes. Margaret announced that she was going home, an expression that she used when going to see her grandfather, John Nally. He recalled briefly seeing her at 6.30. 8 pm was the last time that anyone is known to have definitely seen her alive.

Meanwhile, at her parents' house, they were beginning to worry. At 8 pm, her father took the route that she probably would have taken, travelling along Formosa Street, Shirland Road, Blomfield Road, into Maida Vale, through Lions' Mews and thus into Carlisle Street. He hoped he might see her coming in the other direction. He did not do so. On enquiring at his relatives' homes, he was told that his daughter had departed at 8 pm. So he tried an alternative route home. This was via Clifton Road and Bristol Gardens.

Unable to find her, he went to the service flats for which he was a night porter. At 10 pm, his wife went there to tell him that she still had not returned. The police stations at John Street and Paddington Green were informed of her disappearance. Enquiries were made at infirmaries for the girl.

By 2.30 am, the brutal truth was known to the Nally family. At 11.50 pm, Inspector Richard Groves, a railway official, went around on his duties at Aldersgate Underground station (since 1968 renamed the Barbican). The last train had arrived at the station, so it was time to check the station was clear and then to lock up. He was just checking the cloakrooms. There were two compartments. The right-hand door, the one to the ladies' lavatory, did not seem to open. There was some form of obstruction preventing his entry. He forced the door open and then saw the shocking reality.

It was the corpse of Margaret Nally. Both the City of London police and the Metropolitan police investigated. Margaret had been murdered by having a piece of pique cloth thrust down her throat. The cloth had been torn and was jagged, and this had not been done recently. It measured ten inches by eight, a white, soiled rag. Her drawers and underwear had been torn. There was a slight bruise on her face. But there was even worse to come. She had also been 'terribly assaulted' to use the phrase of the time. A violent sexual attack had occurred.

Edward Nicholls, later a Detective Chief Inspector in the City police, wrote:

> Nobody but a police officer like myself can realise the shock of horror which permeates the whole force on the discovery that a dear little innocent child has been brutally done to death.

Margaret was tall for her age. She had blue eyes, a full face and brown

George Stephenson's *Rocket* at Newcastle station. Author's collection

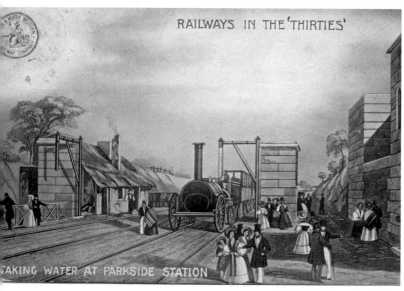

RAILWAYS IN THE 'THIRTIES'

TAKING WATER AT PARKSIDE STATION

One of the first trains, 1830s. Author's collection

Steam train, 1930s. Author's collection

The scene of the crime, 1900s.
Author's collection

Metropolitan
policeman, *c.*1914.
Author's collection

London Bridge, 2009. Author

Folkestone harbour.
Author's collection

London's financial
hub, c.1890s.
Reg Eden's collection

Clapton Square,
2009. Author

Nelson Square, 2009. Author

Hackney church, 2009. Author

St George's Street, 2009. Author

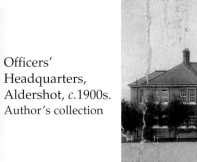

Officers'
Headquarters,
Aldershot, *c.*1900s.
Author's collection

BLEAK HOUSE, BROADSTAIRS.
(WITH PORTRAIT OF CHARLES DICKENS.)

Charles Dickens and his Kent home, 1860s.
Author's collection

Waterloo station, 2009. Author

Brighton railway
station, *c.*1900.
Author's collection

Edward VII, 1900s.
Author's collection

Charing Cross station, *c.*1900.
Author's collection

Paddington station, *c.*1900.
Author's collection

Ludgate station,
*c.*1900. Author's
collection

Windsor High Street
and Castle, 1900s.
Author's collection

Tower of London,
*c.*1900. Author's
collection

Winchester, 1900s.
Author's collection

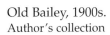

Old Bailey, 1900s.
Author's collection

Portsmouth Town Hall, c.1900. Author's collection

Vauxhall Bridge, 2009. Author

South Croydon station, 2009. Author

Lavender Hill,
2009. Author

Newcastle railway
station, 1900s.
Author's collection

Grey Street, Newcastle, 1900s. Author's collection

Morpeth, 1900s. Author's collection

Lovers in a train carriage, 1900s. Author's collection

Crawley High Street, 1900s. Author's collection

Electric train
on the
Metropolitan
line, *c.*1910.
Author's
collection

Victoria railway
station, 1920s.
Author's
collection

Lewes, 1900s.
Author's
collection

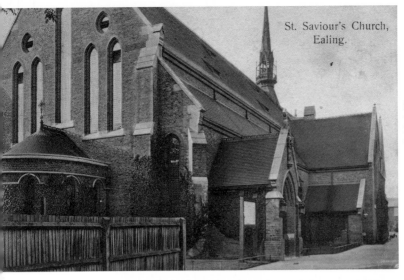

St Saviour's church,
Ealing, 1900s.
Reg Eden's collection

Florence Shore's
grave, 2009.
Author

Homerton
Terrace, 2009.
Author

Deptford Park gates, 2009. Author

Liverpool Street station, 1920s. Author's collection

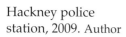

Hackney police station, 2009. Author

Tottenham Court
tube station, 2009.
Author

Train at Carlisle
railway station.
Author's collection

Train arriving at
Basingstoke
station, c.1960.
Author's collection

Cambridge Hospital, Aldershot. Author's collection

The Cambridge Hospital, Aldershot

Bognor Regis, 1950s. Author's collection

Memorial plaque at Russell Square tube station to victims of 2005 terrorist bombing, 2009. Author

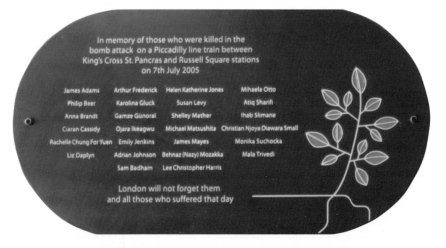

In memory of those who were killed in the
bomb attack on a Piccadilly line train between
King's Cross St. Pancras and Russell Square stations
on 7th July 2005

James Adams	Arthur Frederick	Helen Katherine Jones	Mihaela Otto
Philip Beer	Karolina Gluck	Susan Levy	Atiq Sharifi
Anna Brandt	Gamze Gunoral	Shelley Mather	Ihab Slimane
Ciaran Cassidy	Ojara Ikeagwu	Michael Matsushita	Christian Njoya Diawara Small
Rachelle Chung For Yuen	Emily Jenkins	James Mayes	Monika Suchocka
Liz Daplyn	Adrian Johnson	Behnaz (Nazy) Mozakka	Mala Trivedi
	Sam Badham	Lee Christopher Harris	

London will not forget them
and all those who suffered that day

hair tied up with a pink ribbon. She was wearing a grey coat with a blue half-collar. There were two metal buttons and two side pockets. She wore a white pinafore with a bright coloured sash. She had a dark red frock with a pearl button at the back and wore black shoes and black socks. And she also had a grey blue felt hat, which was trimmed with white.

However, there were few clues. Her hat was not found anywhere. It may have been taken by the killer as a trophy. The police hoped to locate it. A photograph of a similar hat was taken and this was distributed across London. One possibility was that the killer might have decoyed Margaret first taking her to a cinema and the hat was left behind there. However, none of the managers of any of the cinemas in Edgware reported finding one. A halfpenny was found under the body. This might have been used by the killer to decoy the girl away, and thus this would presume he was a stranger to her. Yet, since her pockets were shallow and as she had been given a coin by her aunt, this had probably dropped out of her pocket in the struggle. The cloth which had suffocated her was also seen as a clue. It was not at first thought to be the property of the victim nor her parents. It might have once belonged to the killer. It might have been used as a makeshift handkerchief. It might have been part of a man's shirt or a woman's underclothing. There were marks of blood and teeth on it, suggesting the victim had bitten her attacker and so the man who was being looked for may have been bitten on the hand or wrist.

Railway tickets issued at underground stations for travel were handed in to a ticket collector standing at the entrance once a journey had been completed. So the police examined those given up at Edgware Road and Aldersgate, both singles and returns. Nothing of value was found unfortunately.

Dr Bernard Spilsbury (1877–1947), a well-known Home Office pathologist, undertook a post mortem examination of the body. He thought that the time of death was at about 10 pm on Sunday evening. He and Dr Robert Kearsey, the City police surgeon, also thought that the assault on her had taken place either at the time of her death or shortly afterwards. The two doctors disagreed about the contents of the victim's stomach. She had eaten mutton and giblets for her lunch at home, that was certain, but Spilsbury thought that she might have had a later meal – one given to her by her killer – but his colleague thought it was more likely that the evidence pointed to a case of indigestion, not a second meal.

Rumours and false leads abounded. One was that an old man was seen talking to Margaret in Carlisle Street, but this had no foundation in truth. Another concerned a man who was giving children pudding in Burne Street, a continuation of Carlisle Street, but it transpired that this occurred on the evening after the murder.

Chief Detective Inspector Ottaway of the City police was in charge of the investigation. He heard a number of statements from transport officials which might be relevant. The first was from an omnibus conductor on the bus from Pound Lane to London Bridge. He said that he noticed a soldier aged 30 and a little girl, whom he identified as Margaret, on Sunday at 8.40. The soldier was five feet eight or nine, sallow complexion, medium build, looked ill, had brown hair and a moustache and several days of hair growth. They had got on his bus at the corner of Chapel Street and Edgware Road. The man pushed the girl onto the bus. He was looking a little drunk and she seemed reluctant to accompany him. The man seemed confused about where he wanted to travel to. The girl was without a hat. The two alighted at the corner of Gray's Inn Road. The man led the girl across the road and towards King's Cross station. They stopped at a whelk stall. Then the bus went on its way and that was the last the conductor saw of them. Mr Burwick, the stall holder, did not remember seeing the two. If the soldier was the killer, then they could have reached Aldersgate station from there within minutes, travelling via Euston Square.

Another statement was from a railway guard who was on the Metropolitan railway on the night of the murder. He saw a girl who he thought was Margaret leaving an Edgware Road train at Aldersgate. It was 9.45 and she was accompanied by a woman who was aged between 32 and 35, five feet three inches, respectably dressed in dark clothes and wore a dark flat hat. She appeared to be working class. She helped the hatless girl off onto the platform. The assistant guard did not recollect seeing the girl and the porter did not recall her either. In any case, the crime had been committed by a man. Another witness claimed to have seen Margaret in south London, but this was deemed a case of misidentity.

The inquest on 7 April was held at the City Coroners' Court, Golden Lane Court. Dr Waldo presided. It was well attended. The corpse was to be preserved in the mortuary so people could view it in case it triggered any recollections of that fatal Sunday evening. Both the victim's parents spoke, though her mother broke down in tears. Yet she was pressed to speak and finally examined the cloth which had been thrust into her daughter's mouth. It had come from her daughter's own clothing. Margaret's little friend was asked if she saw her with a strange man on leaving her, but she merely said that she went away alone.

After this, the inquest was adjourned until 22 April. Railway officials at Aldersgate station gave their evidence as has already been described. Yet Edward Spencer, a porter there, gave additional information. He described a man he had seen lurking near the ladies' cloakroom about six or seven weeks before the murder. This man was 32 or 34, five feet seven, with dark hair and a moustache and a thin face. He looked like a builder's labourer, wearing a grey overcoat, a muffler and a black cloth cap. Could this man have been the same as the soldier seen with Margaret on the bus on the evening of the murder? There are certainly similarities in the descriptions given. Detective Inspector Thomas told the court that there had been seven alleged sightings of an adult with a child who looked like Margaret on the night of her death. Clearly, most could not be of her. He added that her hat had still not been found. Finally, a good photograph of the girl had been obtained and was to be distributed throughout London. Medical evidence of the girl having had at least one meal prior to death was given. Yet the depressing conclusion was inevitably given at the end of proceedings – murder by person or persons unknown.

The principal theory of what had happened was thus. A man had taken Margaret on or near Carlisle Street. They had then travelled by train from Edgware Road, the nearest underground station to Carlisle Street, or, perhaps, from Royal Oak, and travelled on the Metropolitan line eastwards, through five stations before stopping at Aldersgate. Yet as she left Carlisle Street at 8 pm and did not arrive at Aldersgate until 10 pm, how is the time to be accounted for, such a train journey would only have taken about 15 minutes. Some of the time could have been spent in Margaret walking back home, but most of it might have been spent with her killer in an Edgware cinema or in a restaurant.

Once at Aldersgate, it was thought that it would have been easy for someone to have slipped into the cloakroom without anyone noticing them. Only the porter might see someone and he might not be on the platform at that time. Nor was there a cloakroom attendant on that duty that evening (he was at Farringdon station from 7.30 pm). There would be few passengers on Sunday evening too. This meant that a man could have easily have slipped into the cloakroom unobserved. Once the girl had been taken into the cloakroom, any screams would have been stifled and nothing of what had happened would have been observed by anyone.

The police appealed to anyone who was travelling on that stretch of the Metropolitan line from 8 to 11 pm on the Sunday evening, and who had seen a man and a child, to come forward. They also wanted to see a man who was of medium height, fresh complexion, clean-shaven and dark haired, who had tried to abduct an 11-year-old in Barnsbury, two days before this murder. Could he have been the killer? The police worked hard, as Nicholls related: 'Hundreds of alleged clues were followed after; days and nights on end were spent in an attempt to track the criminal. It was the biggest manhunt in the City of London.'

Margaret's killer was never found. He had certainly taken a risk in taking his victim by the Metropolitan line to Aldersgate, though there were few people travelling that evening, so the risk was diminished. It is also worth noting that no one sought to blame the parents for allowing their young daughter to walk about a mile through London's streets, unaccompanied. Generally speaking it was completely safe enough to do so. Child murders in London in this era (such as the killing of Marie Bailes in 1908, Willie Starchfield in 1914 and Vera Page in 1931) were extremely rare. Unfortunately, sexual perverts were not entirely unknown even then and it was very unfortunate that Margaret met one of these and went with him, unprotesting and unknowingly, to her doom. The murder may have been planned and Aldersgate selected because it would be a quiet and secluded place to commit such a heinous crime and escape unscathed. It is presumed that she did not know her killer, but this cannot be verified. Was he the soldier on the omnibus that Sunday or was he the man seen at the station weeks previously – assuming the two were not the same? Or was he someone wholly different who came and went unreported by anyone? It seems we shall never know the answer.

Nicholls outlined the difficulty facing the police. 'The man seldom murders twice, and there is no precedent in his methods, and generally speaking, there is a lack of previous planning.' There were certainly no clues to his identity. He concluded:

The crime was undoubtedly the work of a man who though he knew what he was about and that he was doing wrong, was nevertheless impelled by mental disease and an irresistible impulse to commit that diabolical and criminal act. It was a case of the ancient and dangerous and 'uncontrollable impulse'.

11

Death of 'the White Queen', 1920

'She has had a nasty knock of some kind.'

Florence Nightingale Shore was, like her more famous relation (and godmother), a nurse. Her late father was Offley Bohun Shore of Norton Hall, near Sheffield, and cousin to the 'Lady with the Lamp'. Miss Shore was born in Boston, Lincolnshire, in 1865. Her brother was Brigadier General Offley Shore, CB, DSO, and late of the Indian Army, having fought in France during the recent war. He was living in California in 1920, presumably for health reasons. Unmarried, and without any near relations in Britain (her parents were both dead), she was almost alone in the world. She was well travelled and well educated, but a mystery to many of her colleagues. She had had a long and varied career in civil and military nursing. During the First World War, she had been in the Queen Alexandria Imperial Nursing Home Reserve and had served in France. Among the men she treated were black soldiers from France's empire and they called her 'the white Queen'. Demobilized in November 1919, she began living at the Hammersmith and Fulham District Nursing Association Nursing Home at Carnforth Lodge, Queen Street, Hammersmith. Although she had no close friends there, she and Miss Mabel Rogers, the matron, were old friends, and had been so for over 26 years. Miss Rogers later said, 'she was very reserved and very quiet, but cheerful'.

At the beginning of 1920, she was clearly in need of some respite. On Sunday 11 January, she travelled to Tonbridge Wells to see her aunt, the Baroness Farina, returning to Hammersmith on the same day. She had arranged with some friends in St Leonard's to stay with them for a few days, and would meet them at Warrior Square station in St Leonard's. Travelling with Miss Rogers to Victoria station, on Monday 12 January 1920, they arrived at 3.02. The train she planned to take arrived shortly afterwards. Miss Rogers then helped her friend choose an empty compartment, opting for the second one they came to. The time was 3.10. Miss Shore took a corner seat, facing the direction of travel, in a third class non-smoking compartment of the 3.20 train. The carriage was the one at the back of the train. Miss Rogers and Miss Shore entered the compartment. Miss Rogers later said:

> After we had been seated for a little time, a man got in [at 3.17]. He was about 28 or 30, clean shaven and respectable looking. He was wearing a brownish tweed suit of rather mixed and light material. I did not notice the kind of hat he wore, but he had no overcoat. I do not think he had any luggage, but he might have had a small hand bag.

He looked like a bank clerk or a shop assistant. Just before the train was about to depart, the young man offered to help Miss Rogers from the compartment, but she refused his offer. The man was a stranger to both ladies. At this time the window was down.

The train travelled non-stop to Lewes. This was a trip of about 50 miles and the train passed through several long tunnels en route. Although the train slowed down at Gatwick and the Three Bridges, its speed there was still 30 mph, hardly slow enough for a man to depart safely. It arrived at Lewes, at 4.34 (two minutes late). The next station was Polegate Junction, where the train split; some coaches travelling to Eastbourne and the other to Hastings, via Bexhill. No one saw anything odd at the station. At Polegate, George Cloutt, Ernest Thomas and William Ransom, three platelayers employed by the railway company, entered the same compartment as Miss Shore, having finished work at 4.30. They got into the compartment as soon as the train arrived at the station. It was 5 pm. No one could have left the compartment at that station, therefore.

At first, none of the men noticed anything about the middle-aged lady who was apparently asleep in the compartment they were now sharing. She appeared to have dropped her book into her lap and was in a sitting position. In any case, the light in the carriage – incandescent gas – was poor and the weather outside was dark and raining. The window was now pulled up and the blinds had been pulled down down. Cloutt later recalled, 'I saw someone there in the further right hand corner facing the engine'.

It was halfway between Polegate and Bexhill that they first noticed that something might be wrong. Cloutt recalled, 'I saw there was something wrong with her, from the position in which she was.' He said to Ransom, 'She has had a nasty knock of some kind.' They did not think it was too serious; she was breathing and her eyes were open. Cloutts thought she was reading.

However, when the train pulled into Bexhill, at about 5.20, the men contacted Henry Duck, the guard: 'There appears to be something doing up there.' Together, they found there was blood on her clothing and a severe injury to the left side of her head. According to the guard:

> She was in a sloping position facing the engine. The head was back on the padding, and her legs were pushed forward and showing to her knees, because of her having slipped down. Her hands were in front of her and her fingers kept moving. She put out one hand several times, her fingers moved and she appeared to be looking at her hands.

It was decided that she was so badly hurt that she should not be taken off at Bexhill, but should remain on the same train and be taken to the East Sussex Hospital at Hastings.

He travelled with the injured woman for the rest of the journey. The two suitcases she had as her luggage were intact and on the rack above her head. There were broken spectacles and a fancy hair comb on the floor and her leather attaché case had been opened. Her fur hat was on the seat next to her; it was found to have had a gash in it.

Meanwhile, Miss Shore's friend, waiting at Warrior Square station, met the 5.32 train and the 6.45 one, but since Miss Shore did not alight from either, she went home. A telegram was sent to Miss Rogers, who was at the theatre that evening. She took the 11.20 train from Victoria and then motored down from Tonbridge. She arrived at the Hastings hospital on the following day. She remained there for the next few days, until the end. Baroness Farina also visited her niece. Although the doctors and surgeons there tried to save her life, they were unsuccessful. On 7.55 on the morning of 16 January, Miss Shore died, without ever having regained consciousness and the mystery of who killed her deepened even more. Miss Rogers paid her friend a fulsome tribute:

Miss Shore was one of the most unselfish nurses I have ever known. When the hospitals were being bombed by Gothas [German aircraft], she was advised to take shelter. 'No, I never leave my patients' and she remained with the men, walking up and down the ward, speaking cheerful words to them and keeping up their spirits.

The funeral took place at St Saviour's church on The Grove in Ealing on 20 January. This was because she had friends living there and was well known to some of the nurses who worked at St Faith's Nursing Home in Mount Park Road, Ealing. When she had been in London she often attended St Saviour's and it was assumed that her wish would be that the funeral service be held there. There had been a requiem at Christ Church, St Leonard's, before the body had been brought to Ealing. The burial took place at Westminster Cemetery, Hanwell, in the grave where her younger sister had been buried a few years previously. Many people lined the route from the church to the cemetery and the church was packed full. The coffin was draped in the Union flag and there were many floral tributes heaped on it, some from nursing organizations. Police on horse and foot were present for crowd control.

Although the combined police forces of Scotland Yard, the Hastings Borough police and the Sussex Constabulary were involved in this case, they found little in the way of clues. The line from Victoria to Lewes was searched in case the criminal had flung his weapon out of the train. Nothing relevant was found. However, a khaki handkerchief was located near the line at Wivelsfield, but if this had any connection with the case, it was not obvious. They also asked that any tailors, launderers, pawnbrokers and sellers of second clothes should report any bloodstained clothes to them.

No obvious suspect emerged. There was a story about a man who bought a drink in a Lewes pub with a bloodstained pound note. Was he the killer? Then a Lewes barber claimed he cut a man's hair on the day of the attack, and the client resembled the description of the man in Miss Shore's compartment. One man was arrested in Hastings on a charge of burglary a few days after the murder and was found to have an unloaded revolver with a bloodstained butt in his possession (the murder could have been committed using a weapon of this type). He could not account for his movements on the day of the murder and the clothing he had worn at that time had subsequently been destroyed.

Although a railway official thought that a man looking like him left the train at Hastings on the day of the murder, no one else identified him, so he was not thought to be guilty, however. Finally another man tried to leave the country who had a passing resemblance to the suspected man, but was soon cleared.

At the inquest, which was begun at Hastings Hospital on 19 January, what little evidence there was was examined. First, though, the coroner, Mr W J Glenister, paid tribute to the victim, describing her thus 'a lady of philanthropic disposition a nurse of many years' standing'. The jury saw the corpse at the mortuary. They also expressed their sympathy. Miss Rogers told of her escorting her friend to the station and of the young man in the compartment. She then wondered if her friend's appearance was a possible reason for her death. She said:

> Miss Shore was wearing a new fur coat and looked nicely dressed, and I expect that the assailant – whether it was the man in the same compartment I couldn't say – thought she was well off.

If this was the case, then the thief/killer would have been disappointed. The only money she had with her were three one pound notes, and these were missing. On the other hand, the thief did leave the gold rings on her fingers and the brooches in her possession. Jewellery in her case was also left. However, these items might have been difficult and dangerous to dispose of. If this were not the motive, it is unclear what was, for, as Miss Rogers stated, her friend had no enemies. One possibility was that the man was mentally deficient. The only obvious gainer by her death was Brigadier Clarence James Hobkirk, presumably a relation. Miss Shore's will left him a large sum: £14,279 18s 5d. She was the richest person ever to have been killed on a train. It is not thought that the brigadier had any involvement at all in her death.

After Miss Rogers's evidence had been given, the inquest was adjourned until 4 February and was not concluded until 4 March at Hastings Town Hall. There was some discussion as to whether the jury should view the compartment where the crime occurred, but this was decided against.

Henry Duck, the guard on the train, recalled that he had seen a man alight at Lewes. He had come from one of the rear carriages – possibly the one in which Miss Shore had travelled. He jumped from his compartment and walked along the track and then up the platform, clearly in a hurry to leave. Apparently, 'He had a dark, drab mackintosh coat on and I think he wore a cap, but I am not certain'. Duck did not see the man's face. He was about five feet eight and aged between 26 and 30. But Duck paid little attention to him because at that time there was no reason why he should. It did not seem likely that this was the same man as Miss Rogers had seen at Victoria, though there were some similarities.

Spilsbury was once again called upon to examine the corpse on 18 January and gave the jury the benefit of his findings. He said that the deceased was five feet three and well nourished. There were three wounds to the head. Death had been due to a coma because the skull had been fractured and the brain had been damaged. According to Spilsbury, these injuries 'were caused by very severe blows by a heavy instrument having a fairly large striking surface'. She had been struck whilst she was seated. Possibly the butt of a revolver had been used to injure her. He added that there was no sign of any sexual interference or any attempt at the same.

The last sitting of the inquest lasted two hours and fifty minutes. It was noted that the police had questioned ten men and had taken statements from at least 100 people. There were many more tributes to the deceased. There were hopes expressed that an arrest would be made. The jury could only make the verdict that this was a case of murder by person or persons unknown.

It seemed fairly certain that the murder occurred between Victoria and Lewes and that the killer probably left the train at the latter, the first stop after Victoria. Clearly he was not in the compartment at Polegate, since he did not leave there, according to the platelayers; so he must have alighted at the previous station – Lewes. The killing must have taken place some time before Lewes was reached, because the man had had time to rearrange his victim's body to make it look as if she was asleep; giving him more time to escape before the hue and cry was raised.

The train was a long one, of eleven carriages, and was longer than the relatively short platform then at Lewes station. The passengers in the two back carriages, if they wished to alight there could wait until the train moved on a little. Or they could simply leave and walk along the track and on the platform at the latter's end, as the killer, eager to escape, would have done.

The next question is, after he left the train at Lewes, what did he do next? He could have taken a return train to Victoria. Or he could have travelled on by another train, to Brighton. Or, as the train split at Polegate, he could have joined the forward portion of the train which was bound for Eastbourne. Or he could have just left the station there and gone into Lewes proper by going over the railway fences to the junction of Station Road and Friars' Walk. Mr Marchant, the stationmaster, ridiculed this idea because he thought it would have brought more attention to the man, which he would have wanted to avoid. None of the railway staff noticed anything obviously unusual, but then none of them was aware that a brutal assault had just occurred on the train. Although the line was normally busy, on this dark and wet day, which was not in the tourist season, there were not many travellers.

Mr McMaster MP asked the Minister of Transport what was being done to prevent crimes of this nature. He was told that the railway companies provided designated compartments for 'ladies only' and female passengers would be made aware of this option.

It seems highly probable that the man seen by Miss Rogers in the same compartment as Miss Shore must have been the killer. No one else had entered, and there was no one else there after the train left Lewes. The motive was certainly robbery. He was ready to commit an assault, having a weapon with him already, and took the opportunity to attack his victim, as she was alone and thus vulnerable. He struck, taking her completely by surprise, and left at his first opportunity, but whoever he was, he easily escaped.

It has also been suggested that Miss Rogers was the killer, presumably inventing the man seen in Miss Shore's compartment, which we only have her word for, but the motive is unclear.

12

A Crime of Passion, 1927

'I have killed my girl. I have stabbed her in one of these compartments, I don't know which.'

Passion, in all its forms, as well as financial gain, has been a common motive for murder. It is usually easy to detect, for either the criminal acts without thought to evade the police, as in Chapter 10, or confesses. Furthermore, the killer is someone well known to the victim and so will be a name which crops up as the police begin to talk to their family and friends. This case is no exception to the general rule.

Daisy Dorothy Mays was aged 25 in 1927 and was a typist, employed at Ortweiler's works in East London and lived at Grinstead Road, Deptford. She had 'been keeping company' with one James Frederick Stratton. He was a 26-year-old warehouse packer who lived in Homerton Terrace, Homerton. His history was not an altogether happy one. He had been born on 10 February 1901 in Hackney. His mother, Ada Marion Stratton, had died of appendicitis when he was 6 months old. James was looked after by his grandmother, Mrs Mary Padley, and he lived with her throughout his life. James attended the London County Council School on Chatham Place, Hackney, until he left, aged 14, in 1915. He had an unexceptional record there. His working life began in a Hackney printing firm for a few months. Then he worked for Mr Marsh, a confectioner, at Bethnal Green, again, for a few months. From about 1916 he was employed by a woollen goods merchant near Aldersgate Street. Then, from 1919, he worked as a warehouse packer at Mr Ortweiler's, a fancy leather goods merchant, whose works was based at Great Arthur Street, Golden Lane, EC. It was undoubtedly here that he and Daisy met. In 1905, two men by the name of Stratton had killed a shopkeeper and his wife in Deptford (see the author's *Foul Deeds and Suspicious Deaths in Lewisham and Deptford*) – but presumably James was no relation.

His character was variously assessed. According to Mr Ortweiler, he 'was a very good servant and always well behaved'. His 75-year-old grandmother gave a more ambivalent statement, 'her grandson was usually well behaved, but at times gave way to violent fits of temper, also that a few months ago, after having had a argument with his uncle, Stratton threatened to go upstairs, get his revolver and blow out his uncle's brains'. It should be stated, as no gun was ever located, that the threat was likely made more in anger than in any serious intention to carry it out.

His family history, as pointed out already, was not entirely happy. A few more points can be made. First, his father, Frederick, who lived in Richmond Avenue, Southend on Sea, in 1927, had only seen his son twice after 1909. There might also have been some degree of mental instability in the family. Frederick's sister, Deborah McGarth, had shot herself in 1894. His mother had died in 1909 in some kind of institution in Birmingham.

Daisy had not introduced James to her family, as her brother, although he knew of her association with him, did not know his name nor where he lived. In fact, relations between the lovers was deteriorating, although no one quite knew how drastically. Matters came to a crisis in February 1927.

Stratton had hoped to see Daisy on the evening of Sunday 20 February. She did not keep the appointment. He went around to his house in Hackney, but she was not there. He then went to Deptford to try and find her. After walking around some of the streets there, near her home in Grinstead Road, he saw her with another man. Stratton did not make himself known to them and wandered off.

The man in question was one Clement Freeman, a 22-year-old plater's mate, who lived with his parents in Windmill Lane, Deptford. He had known her for seven years, but had been walking out with her since 26 January 1926. He claimed, 'I have seen her practically every night'. They used to meet at Deptford Park Gates, just around the corner from where she lived, Daisy arriving from Shoreditch by the 47 bus and later he would see her home. On that evening, they had met at 6.30 and were together for the next five hours. In this time they went to the New Cross Cinema (on the day before they had been to the Prince of Wales cinema in Lewisham). They arranged to meet on the following evening at the Polytechnic on Regent Street at 10 pm, where Freeman attended the gymnasium.

Initially, Daisy did not tell her new boyfriend about Stratton. She claimed that the weekend afternoons she spent with Stratton were afternoons spent with girlfriends. However, in April 1926, she did begin to tell him about her worries. He said, 'She was afraid he would get to know that she was walking out with me.' In June of that year, Stratton began to make threats. Freeman suggested that she tell her brother, or the police, but she did neither. Yet by early 1927, Daisy thought life was looking up, as Freeman stated, 'Daisy had seemed happier than ever since Christmas and I took this as a sign that the fellow had left her alone.' This was because, although Stratton threatened her if she did not spend Christmas with him, she had ignored him and spent it with Freeman instead, and apparently Stratton had not carried out his threats. Yet this was to dwell in a fool's paradise.

On Monday 21 February, Stratton was at work. In the morning, he asked Edmund Hearn, an errand boy employed by the firm, to take a message to Daisy from him (she was working at the British Industries Fair at White City). The message read as follows:

Dear May,
Must see you tonight, I have some good news for you Jack will be coming along send word back with him what time can you see me at Liverpool Street If you can't I will be there at 7.30 and stay till you come, Don't fail
Jim

Stratton pledged the lad to secrecy, telling him, 'Will you give this to Miss Mays? Don't let anyone else up there see it, or they might turn funny.' That afternoon, at one, he asked John Welch, another colleague, who drove lorries for the firm, if he could ask Daisy if she had a message for him. Since he was driving towards White City that afternoon, it was no trouble for him. They arranged to meet that night at Liverpool Street station at 7.30. At 1.45 that afternoon, he went home and gave his grandmother some money. He then left, with murder in mind, as he later said, to 'get ready to do Daisy in'. He met Sidney Cameron, an old friend, and they went to the Prince of Wales pub for a drink and played bagatelle there. Then Stratton told Cameron, 'I feel queer, I am going out for a walk and may see you later'. He did not tell Cameron where he was going. Meanwhile, Daisy left White City at 7 pm.

That night, Stratton and Daisy met by appointment and travelled from Broad Street station, which was to the immediate west of Liverpool Street station, and handled suburban North London traffic, to Hackney by train (on the London, Midland and Scottish Railway). Perhaps Daisy hoped the meeting would be short so that she could then meet Freeman later that night – clearly she thought she had the situation in control, a fatal mistake, because she was unaware that Stratton knew that she was seeing another man. Leaving the station, Stratton went to the Pelican pub for a drink, leaving Daisy briefly in the street. They met on the platform again and boarded a third class compartment on the next train. Stratton took her to task over why she had not seen him the night before. She lied: 'I stayed in because it was raining.' Stratton replied: 'If you want to go home anymore, you have got to tell me the truth.' He then asked her who the man she had been with was. Daisy answered, 'I was not with any fellow and I have not been with anyone.' Stratton knew that this was a lie and it was then that he completely lost his temper.

At 8.20 the train stopped between Hackney and Dalston Junction stations because of a signal. It was here that the first outsider was to have any inclination at all that something was amiss. Walter Tidd, the train's fireman noticed Stratton walking along the track. The following conversation ensued, with Tidd asking,

'What is the matter?'

'Take me to the police. I have killed a girl.'

'Come along with me.'

'I hope she is dead.'

'Why?'

'Because if she is not it will mean 10 years for me. I have killed my girl. I have stabbed her in one of these compartments, I don't know which, one of these chaps will tell you because they have heard her scream.' The 'chaps' referred to included John Poole and Frederick Griffiths, two clerks who were on their way to their evening class in Dalston.

Tidd took Stratton to the guard, George Blackmore, and told him Stratton's story. They took him to the stationmaster's office (at Dalston Junction station) and then sent for a doctor and the police. They also noticed that Stratton's hands were bloodstained. Meanwhile, Joseph Poole, another railway employee, went to the compartment and found Daisy's bloodstained corpse. He also found a piece of iron wrapped in brown paper and cloth. Constables Johnson and Hart were the first to arrive, the former leaving point duty on Graham Road to do so. A description of the murder scene was provided by PC John Hart:

I saw the body of a woman lying on the floor between the seats, the head was towards the platform lying against the right seat. A woman's hat was lying on the seat, also a leather music case [which contained Stratton's earlier note to her] and an umbrella, a piece of iron wrapped in cloth and covered with blood was lying by the feet and a knife, also covered with blood was lying by the head. A small piece of brown paper was lying near the bar of iron. The woman's clothes was covered with blood, there were wounds in the front of the throat and the floor of the carriage was covered in blood.

Dr Homes was called and saw the corpse. He gave an official pronouncement of death. After the body was taken to the mortuary, it was examined by Dr Barlow, the divisional surgeon, and he noted that there were 24 wounds.

Stratton was taken to Hackney Police Station. On the following day he was officially charged with the murder of Dorothy Mays. He elaborated with a further statement:

We have been keeping company for about 7 or 8 years. Since Christmas I have noticed a change in her affections towards me and I was determined that if I could not have her nobody else should and I have been awaiting a favourable opportunity 'to do her in'.

When the two were alone in a compartment on the carriage of a North London train, the opportunity had arisen. Stratton took his chance:

I then pulled the piece of iron out of my pocket and struck her several times on the head with it. She fell to the floor of the carriage and I then pulled out the knife and stabbed her several times. The train then stopped, as the signal was against it. I jumped out of the carriage and slammed the door, walking along to the driver of the train, and told him to call the police as I had murdered my girl. The fireman got off his engine and took me to Hackney railway station.

On 25 February, the inquest was held at Bethnal Green Coroners' Court. Stratton wanted to attend and he was granted permission from the prison governor to do so. Because of his injury on the previous day to his left hand, his arm was in a sling. Otherwise, he was described thus 'a tall, good looking man of rather pale complexion'. John James May, brother of the deceased, identified her body. Dr Barlow, the divisional police surgeon, told the court that he had found ten wounds to the head, a severe bruise to the left ear, five punctures to the neck, and eight stab wounds in the middle of her back, below the shoulder blades. There was no evidence of any struggle. The jury concluded that this was a case of murder by Stratton.

The magistrates' court, meeting on 1 March, sent Stratton for trial at the Old Bailey. The accused made no statement as the prosecuting counsel, Mr Clark, said that this was 'a very cruel type of murder'. At the Old Bailey on 10 March, Stratton pleaded guilty. His defence counsel, Edward Pule, said that the crime was due to a serious mental abnormality, even though Hugh Grierson, prison doctor at Brixton, thought that Stratton was sane enough. He was found guilty and had nothing to say as to why he should not be executed. The death sentence was duly passed.

The force of the law acted quickly. There was thought to be no reason why the Home Secretary should advise the King to grant a reprieve. On 29 March 1927, at 9 am, Mr R Baxter of Balfour Street, Hertford, executed Stratton at Brixton prison. According to the inquest on Stratton's body, 'Death [was] due to dislocation of cervical vertebrae by hanging executed by law.'

This had been yet another case of obsessive love turning violent. Daisy had tried to break away from Stratton, by turning to Freeman. Unfortunately, this had led to dire consequences when Stratton found that she had been seeing another man. Stratton prepared himself to kill her. Finally, when she lied twice to him, he was unable to hold himself back and his anger became fatal for both of them.

13

Murder on the Underground, 1939

'A sudden impulse came over me and I wanted to push
someone under the train.'

Avril Ray Waters seemed to be an ordinary girl. She had been born on 31 March 1924 and lived with her parents in Broadfields Avenue, Edgware. Her father, Eric Knowles Waters, was the manager of a grocery in Edgware. Miss Waters had left school and in 1939 was learning secretarial skills at a Pitman's College in London. She travelled there by tube, presumably on the Bakerloo line and changing to the Central line.

On the evening of 15 February, she had finished her studies for the day there and was standing on platform 4 of the Tottenham Court tube station. It was the rush hour and the platform was crowded with hundreds of people. Bernard Wilson Whiting was driving the train which was approaching the platform. He later told the police:

On 15th February 1939, at 5.04 pm I was driving an electric train into Tottenham Court Railway Station. At about 100 feet from the head wall of the west bound platform, I saw what appeared to be a woman falling in front of my train. I applied the emergency brakes at once and stopped, but went over the body for one and a half cars' length. I got underneath and found a girl one and a half cars down, hanging feet downwards on the centre rail. She was on her stomach.

Just a moment before, Dr Robert Fisher had been among the waiting passengers. He recalled:

I was sitting down reading. I folded my paper as a train came in.

Just to my left and between me and the train a girl was standing. I noticed somebody push her and dash through the entrance almost directly behind. The girl screamed and fell in front of the train.

Edwin Hunt, the lift man employed at the station, saw the girl fall and the running man. He chased after him and caught up with him. His quarry said, 'I didn't mean it.' Another member of railway staff joined Hunt. He was told by Hunt, 'You had better take charge of this man as he has admitted pushing somebody on the line.' Hunt added, 'He was very much upset. I can't say if he was sweating.'

It appeared the man was sick. Dr Fisher witnessed the capture of the assailant and then he went to see if he could help Miss Waters. He assisted in removing her to the platform and remained with her until the ambulance arrived. He administered morphine and helped her be taken up the escalator on a stretcher. By 5.45 the ambulance had taken her to Charing Cross Hospital. Dr Thomas McKelvey tried to help her, but she was beyond medical care and died there at 6.05. Her father was called upon to identify his daughter, which he did at 8 pm. Dr McKelvey then performed a post mortem. He concluded, 'She died as a result of shock and haemorrhage from multiple injuries. She had a fractured skull and a severe crushing of the lower spinal vertebrae.'

Back at the scene of the crime, PC David John was the first policeman to arrive. He saw the accused man in the stationmaster's office at about 5.10. One railway official told him, 'This is the man who is supposed to have pushed the girl under the train.' 'Do you hear that?' the constable asked the accused. He replied, 'I don't know. I don't know.' He later said, 'I don't know what made me do it.' He was then taken to Tottenham Court Road Police Station, where he was interviewed under caution by Detective Inspector Peter Beveridge at 10.45.

On the following day, the accused man was formally charged at a magistrates' court. He tried to give his interpretation of events, making the following statement, 'I don't know what made me do it. A sudden impulse came over me and I wanted to push someone under the train. I've been worried because I couldn't get work.'

Who was the accused man who had acted so impulsively and fatally? His name was Leonard Ward Davies, aged 30 and living in Windsor Road, Holloway. Both his parents had been alcoholics and one of his aunts had died in an asylum. On 7 September 1937, he was given a six-month gaol sentence for 'causing a public nuisance' by falsely confessing to a murder. During his incarceration he had tried to commit suicide. On 30 November he was sent to Bexley Heath mental hospital, it being believed he was insane. He was discharged on 5 March 1938.

In the next two months he was employed as a barman at the Archway pub in Holloway. Terrence Mahon, another barman there, recounted a conversation he had had with Davies:

> I recalled that he seemed rather distressed in his mind. At one time he asked me if I believed in people having a split personality. I said my knowledge of psychology was insufficient for me to answer him. He asked me in a nervous tentative sort of way what I would think of a man who had an uncontrollable impulse to throw someone under a train. I believe I replied that no impulse need be uncontrollable if he exercised willpower.

After Davies had been committed for trial for murder at the Old Bailey for 21 March, he was sent to Brixton prison. Whilst there, Dr Hugh Grierson, the senior medical officer, formed his own judgement about him, based on continuous observation and some interviews. Davies conformed to prison routine and seemed unconcerned and unanxious about his own fate, even though he faced death if found guilty. Grierson made the following assessment:

> He says he had to do it. He says a similar impulse came over him 10 minutes earlier when he was at St Paul's station, but he did not act on it. He denies any hallucinations such as voices telling him to do it. He exhibits no regrets nor remorse, and though he does not say so, he gives the impression that he would do it again if given the opportunity. He even has no feelings for the parents of the victim. Both in words and writing he has expressed a lack of feeling and lack of any interest as to the outcome of the trial. I am of the opinion that he is insane and unfit to plead to the indictment.

Given this judgement, on 24 March, Justice Hawke had no hesitation in ordering Davies to be sent to Broadmoor. Miss Waters, like most victims of killers in trains or at stations, was unlucky enough to be in the proximity of a man who was determined to kill. Caught by surprise, she had no chance. Davis was not the first nor the last man with mental problems who was released into the world and who would kill before being incarcerated. He received a conditional discharge on 6 March 1951, but this was revoked and he was readmitted on 7 April 1951. He was briefly at the North Wales Hospital in 1962–3, but returned to Broadmoor, dying there on 16 June 1965.

14

Murder in Wartime, 1942

'I heard a scream, some thuds and a man yelling as if he were laughing.'

Beatrice Nellie Meadmore was aged 61 and a married woman. She had once worked as a buyer for Messrs Peter Robinson Ltd in Oxford Street. She was still working at the time of her death, probably in a shop in Central London, too. Her husband was Otto, director of a Friendly Society. They lived at Barn Rise, Wembley Park.

On Wednesday 25 February 1942, Mrs Meadmore finished work and, as planned, went to the Classic Cinema on Baker Street. She had informed her husband of her intention and he had no problem with this. When the film was finished, she left and went to Baker Street tube station. It was about 8.10 pm when she boarded a northbound Metropolitan line train to take her to Wembley Park station. The train was one which was subdivided into compartments. This was a journey of about thirteen minutes, with only the one stop, at Finchley. She planned to be home at 8.30. The journey from Finchley to Wembley Park took eight minutes due to several delays.

However, just before the train stopped at Wembley Park, a man jumped off the moving train. This was a surprise to a group of three men who were standing on the platform, waiting for the train. One of these three was James Farhill of Harrow, who remarked, 'That's a fine way to get off a train.' The man replied 'yes' and then stumbled when he reached the platform, but soon picked himself back up again and then rushed away to the station's exit.

The three men entered the train compartment which the man had just left so hurriedly and there they saw a woman huddled into a corner. She was groaning and there was a newspaper over her face. At first they assumed she had been drinking. However, one of them became suspicious and called for a member of underground staff, after asking her 'Are you alright?' and presumably receiving no response. Several officials eventually arrived at the still stationary train. They found that the woman was unconscious, having been attacked and then robbed. She was taken to the waiting room and first aid was administered.

An ambulance was summoned and the woman was taken to Wembley Hospital. It was soon ascertained that this was Mrs Meadmore. Her husband, who had returned home from work at 7.15, was told at 9.15 by the police of what had happened. He went to the hospital and kept a vigil by his wife's bedside. Dr John Shipman was the resident medical officer and he saw her on arrival. Her scalp was bloody and he operated on her after anaesthetic was given. However, she died at 6 am on the following day, her husband by her bedside. She only very briefly regained consciousness and said, 'it was a man'.

Spilsbury undertook the post mortem. Death was due to compound fractures of the skull and injuries to the brain. The weapon was a blunt and heavy instrument, perhaps a jemmy, which was never found. The police put out pleas for help in the local newspaper, the *Kilburn Times*. Detective Inspector Deighton was in charge and announced, 'The police want to know if anyone saw a man rush either out of the station or into the other train. He was about five feet eight inches, or five feet nine inches in height, and was wearing a light overcoat, bloodstained and a trilby hat.'

The inquest was held on 3 March, but was adjourned until 9 April, where it was held at St John's School room. There was not much of substance to add to the meagre details already known. A man in the next compartment recalled hearing a noise in the compartment next to his, presumably between Baker Street and Wembley Park. The motive had probably been robbery, because it was thought that there might have been about £3 in her handbag, which was found in the compartment, having been rifled through. It was also thought that the killer was a man in his early thirties.

Frederick Baker, assistant superintendent of the London Transport Passenger Board, had been on the train in question and recounted:

Just as we were passing through West Hampstead station, I heard a scream, some thuds and a man yelling as if he were laughing. I thought it was some youngsters fooling about; and I didn't attach much importance to the noise.

At Wembley Park, he heard a man shouting for a guard. He went to the compartment where the noise was coming from and saw Mrs Meadmore. He also saw the killer escaping and gave chase, but was unable to find him. Dr Cogswell wound up the inconclusive inquest and Detective Inspector Richardson announced that the police would continue their investigation into the murder. They also looked at other instances where women had been attacked on that line in recent times, including one where a female railway clerk had been attacked for money.

The police theory, which seems reasonable enough, was that after the murder the killer had left the compartment at Wembley Park as fast as he could and was the man seen by the three others. He then caught the train on a nearby platform, the 8.21 from Aylesbury, which left Wembley Park at 8.25, and so returned to Central London. It is assumed he took the weapon with him, which must have been a small, but heavy, item, easily concealable in a pocket. A minute search was made of the track between Finchley and Wembley Park, but nothing was found. In all likelihood, he was a complete stranger to Mrs Meadmore. Her husband knew of no one who would want to have injured his wife. He may well have been desperate for any money he could find, and seeing a single and vulnerable woman alone in a railway compartment he took his chance. He may have entered the compartment at Finchley. Anyone who had seen a nervous or agitated man on the train from Aylesbury to Marylebone was urged to contact the police. Whether anyone did or not, the result was inconclusive, for no one was ever charged with this murder.

15

Death at West Croydon Station, 1945

'I had a clear view of his face with a horrible expression
of horror and terror.'

Whilst most attention in April 1945 and the following weeks was upon the international situation, with the imminent defeat of Germany, the suicide of Hitler and Victory in Europe, domestic drama still had its place.

On the Saturday afternoon of 21 April 1945, three people were intent on their own business on the platform of West Croydon station, whilst they awaited the arrival of the next train to London Waterloo. It was about 2.50 pm. The oldest of this trio was Ronald Lonsdale, a 52-year-old factory worker, then residing in Derby Road, Croydon. The others were Frank Hutchinson, a 33-year-old glass blower, 'a thick set, fair haired man', and Margaret, his wife, both of whom hailed from Birkbeck Road, Kendray, in Barnsley. It was the old story of the eternal triangle. This one would end in tragedy.

On this occasion there was a scuffle between the two men. The result was that Lonsdale fell in the direction of the approaching train. Frank Mutter, the driver of the oncoming train recalled seeing him with his arms and legs outstretched and falling in front of the train, 'I had a clear view of his face with a horrible expression of horror and terror.' David Gravotte, a 12-year-old lad, was leaning out of the window and saw the two men struggle, a lunge and then a fall. Lonsdale was killed by being run over by the train. Betty Whitfield, a Battersea librarian, also saw what had happened.

At 8 pm that night, at Croydon Police Station, Detective Inspector Albert Bastable saw Hutchinson, who was 'in a bad state of nerves' and informed him, 'You know who I am. I have seen the body of Ronald Lonsdale, and you will be charged with wilfully murdering him by pushing him under a train at West Croydon station.' Lacking much money, Hutchinson was granted legal aid in order to provide himself with a barrister. Meanwhile he was remanded in custody for 14 days.

The inquest took place on 25 April before Dr Beecher-Jackson, the coroner. The dead man's widow, Mrs Clara Lonsdale, told the jury that her husband left their marital home at Upper Sheffield Road, Barnsley, about nine weeks before, apparently in order to find work in London. However, he only wrote to her at the beginning of April to let her know that he had found a job in Croydon. Dr David Haber, a pathologist, announced that death was due to shock and haemorrhage caused by multiple injuries as inflicted by the train. The inquest was adjourned and the police appealed for any witnesses who could assist them in the investigation.

Much of the background to the case was made public at the magistrates' court hearing at Croydon on 7 May. Mrs Hutchinson had left her family early on 19 February 1945. Initially, her husband did not know where she had gone. In March she wrote to her husband. She was very sorry that she had left him and apologised for the terrible effect on their children that this must have caused. Hutchinson wrote back to her care of Streatham post office. He told her that he forgave her behaviour, asked her to return and hoped that they could have a fresh start. She replied that she could not face her family again after what she had done.

Hutchinson was undeterred. Because of heart troubles, he gave up his glass-blowing job. He was now free to find his wife and seek employment elsewhere. He came down to London in the week before Easter. He was unable to find her, so returned home. Then he tried to find a job in London, so he would have more chance of locating his missing wife. On 16 April, he went to the Powers Automatic Factory in Aurelia Road, Croydon. Here, he asked for Bob Lonsdale, who worked there. Lonsdale saw Hutchinson and said, 'I am glad you have come; Margaret is not well.' The two men arranged to meet at 5.15 pm, after Lonsdale had finished work, in order to pursue their conversation.

The two met and Hutchinson saw his estranged wife. She seemed happy to return to him and they went back to Crofton Park, to live together for the next four days. Yet on 20 April she left him again and returned to where she had been living with Lonsdale in West Croydon. Her husband followed her. She suggested that he should go to Plymouth to find work, while she decided what she should do. Lonsdale was told of this decision. Various discussions took place between the different parties.

On 21 April the three were in a pub at 1 pm; possibly the one at the corner of Derby Road. They had three drinks each, 'we were quite amicable' and then went to West Croydon station, just opposite the pub. This was so that Hutchinson could take a train to Waterloo and then change for a Plymouth train. Mrs Hutchinson then began to walk off. Hutchison later said, 'We went down on the platform and we stood talking. I moved about because I could not keep still, being impatient. I looked around and saw my wife walking off down the platform on her own.' It was then that Mrs Hutchinson made her decision, 'On the platform I decided to go with my husband because I feel sorry for him.' Lonsdale ran after her and brought her back. She was tearful. There was a brief exchange of words between the three, with Lonsdale first addressing Hutchinson: 'She is going back to her digs.'

Mrs Hutchinson replied, 'I think it is better for me to go back to the kids'.

'You can't go back and leave me. I love you too much to go without you'.

Hutchinson then stated, 'Now then, Bob, I have acted like a gentleman. Now be sensible and we will all get on the train.'

'You can't get on the train.'

It was now that the 2.19 train from Epsom was slowing down in order to stop on the platform. It was 2.40 and it was then that Hutchinson pushed Lonsdale and the latter fell in front of the train and was killed. Hutchinson reported the incident to William Tidy, a ticket collector.

Mrs Hutchinson, in court, gave a brief summary of events. She had married Frank in 1934. They had three children since then (in 1945, one was aged 11, one 10 and the youngest was 8). Then the Second World War intervened and, as with so many other women, changed her from being a housewife and mother into a war worker. In 1942 she was working in the same factory as Bob Lonsdale, a married man. They began an affair and, unable to withstand the barbs of local gossips, fled together to Croydon where they were unknown. Mrs Hutchinson made a comment about the fatal afternoon, 'I thought they were going to start fighting and turned away. I heard someone scream – it was all in split second.' She added, 'I was anxious to get my husband back and he wanted his wife back.' The court decided that Hutchinson should be sent for trial at the Old Bailey.

On 7 June, Hutchinson pleaded not guilty to the charge of murder. He stated that his wife had been living with Lonsdale in Croydon and that he came down to see her. He recounted how the three found themselves on the platform at the railway station. Although he admitted to having a brief struggle with Lonsdale there, he insisted that he had not intended to kill him. All three of them had intended to take the train to Waterloo that afternoon, with Hutchinson then going on to Plymouth.

Hutchinson then explained that Lonsdale had tried to stop his wife from boarding the train. Hutchinson then told the court:

> I pushed him and said, 'Get out of the way. We are getting on the train'. I pushed him in such a way that he would fall away from the train. I am quite sure I did not mean to push him onto the train. I wanted to get on it with my wife. At the time I pushed him he was trying to get between us and the edge of the platform to keep us from the train.

The judge announced that a man was entitled to protect his wife, and that Hutchinson had not meant to kill Lonsdale. The jury agreed and found Hutchinson not guilty of murder. He walked from the court a free man.

Was Hutchinson saved from the gallows by the morality of the time? After all, he was seen as the injured party and Lonsdale was guilty as an adulterer and wife snatcher. Clearly, though, Hutchinson had not set out to kill anyone. The worst he should have been charged with was manslaughter, not murder, as there was no intent beforehand. What seems to have happened is that Lonsdale decided to stop the Hutchinsons from boarding the train and there was a scuffle. Hutchinson pushed the older man away. It was Lonsdale's misfortune that he fell in front of the train and was killed. Arguably, this was Hutchinson's fortune, for it removed his rival in his wife's affections. Fortunately for him, the jury was sympathetic towards him, very possibly rightly so.

16

Death of a Railway Servant, 1952

'You know about my previous trouble, don't you?
I did a murder in Germany.'

Despite copious notices on railway stations and trains warning that any assaults on railway staff will be treated most severely, it is unusual for railway staff to be actually killed in the line of duty. Passengers, of course, are another matter. This case is an exception to the general rule to date (another is the shooting of George Gardiner at Kilburn station in December 1942).

Geoffrey Charles Dean was born in Weymouth in 1920. He had been apprenticed as an engineer on leaving school, but the Second World War intervened. During that conflict, he served in the Airborne Division, in operations in Norway in 1940 and at Arnhem in 1944. He was particularly proud of his achievements in the former and kept a framed certificate at home. In 1946 he married Margery Ruth and by 1952 the couple had a 5-year-old daughter. It was said, 'He just lived for his family'. Since 1947 they had lived in a flat in a house on the Guildford Road, Ash, Surrey. From April 1949 he was employed by British Rail and worked at Ash Vale station from February 1951. His brother-in-law described him thus, 'a very quiet, steady, decent fellow, very conscientious at his job'.

The unexpected drama into which he was unwittingly thrust began to unfold on Wednesday 20 August 1952. Norman Thompson was a railway clerk, who had worked at Ash Vale for only 16 days. He was at the station's enquiry desk late that morning, between 11 and 11.30. It was here that one James John Alcott, a young fireman (born on 13 October 1929) employed by the railways for the past year and a half, came to the counter. He asked about local trains from Victoria to Dover.

Alcott returned there on the following day, at about 5 pm. He wanted to use the booking office's telephone. As a railway employee who showed his pass, he was allowed to do so. He rang the Motive Power Department, Bricklayers' Arms Depot, London. The telephone call concerned a fitter called Turner who had been injured in an accident there. The man had been hurt by clinkers thrown out of a passing engine. Alcott said that they would ring him back, but didn't.

Mortimer Harrington, a porter employed at Ash Vale, recalled seeing Alcott in the staff room at 6.30 that evening. The two had a chat, but Alcott didn't mention his injured friend. Harrington had seen Alcott before and presumably felt relaxed with his presence. John Wright, another porter, also spoke to him, and recalled 'he had a sheath knife . . . he was cleaning his nails with it . . . he said he had got it for his young nephew'. No one thought it was unusual for anyone to carry such a weapon, or even, to have it as a present for a young relation. Richard Hill, a signalman, talked with Alcott; the latter speaking about his trips to France to see his wife, who was French. Alcott left before 7.

On Friday 22 August, before going to work, Dean warned his wife that he might be late home because he had some accounts to work on. As on the previous two days, Alcott visited the station. Harrington remembered seeing him using the telephone there at 5.30 pm. Two hours later, he was seen standing by the telephone. Richard Hill was at the booking office answering the telephone.

At a quarter to nine that evening, Kenneth Vincent, an army corporal from the nearby barracks, called at the booking office in order to buy a train ticket. He recalled:

> I went to the booking office window, the booking office window was shut and the window partition was down and I couldn't see in. There was some disturbance going on inside the booking office. It appeared to me not to be too aggressive, it appeared to be the type of sound heard in a barrack room, like two men playing around together. There was a muffled voice but I couldn't discern what it was and couldn't distinguish any words. I had a coin in my hand and I rapped on the till of the window with the coin. There was no response whatsoever and the noise inside continued. I must have stood by the window for half a minute or so.

Vincent evidently gave up on his quest for a ticket and walked away. At 8.55, Cedric Bull, the junior porter, returned to the station after having his supper of fried fish. He went to the booking office, where he noticed that the lights were still on. He then looked through the grill 'and when I looked through I could see Mr Dean's feet and some blood on the floor'. He then raised the alarm, but he and his colleagues were unable to open the door. Bernard Luck, the stationmaster, was at Aldershot. He was told of the situation by Bull by telephone, and he arrived at 9.02. He ordered that the door be broken open and Dean's dead body was found there. There were empty cash bags and keys on the floor. Leonard Marsh, a railway clerk, discovered that a total of £168 1s 11 ^{1}/2d had disappeared. The police began to arrive at 9.30, first PC Cedric Shirer, then his senior colleagues. Dr Arthur Mant, first assistant to the Department of Forensic Medicine at Guy's Hospital, was on the scene at 11.30.

Meanwhile, sometime after 9 pm, a bus took Alcott into Aldershot. He went to a pub, the Rat Pit, and had two pints. He began talking to a woman there. He was looking for accommodation. She took him to Edith Dagger's house in Victoria Road, arriving at 10.20. Mrs Dagger took guests for bed and breakfast. Mrs Dagger recalled, 'He came with a lady.' She asked if Alcott could stay, and was given a bedroom on the first floor for a week. Alcott paid the £2 12s 6d which was demanded. He lacked any kit, but said he was going to France. He signed his name in the guest book and wrote his address following it – Eltham Palace Road, South-East London. Alcott had breakfast there on the following morning, leaving at 9 am. That day he bought a pair of new shoes. He returned at 11.07 pm.

He must have been surprised at who he saw on his return. As part of the police investigation into Dean's death, all boarding houses and hotels in the Aldershot district were being searched. DC William Mann had, coincidentally, arrived at the guest house just after Alcott had left. He searched the house and found, in Alcott's room, his blue jacket. On it were bloodstains. There were two pound notes in it, both covered in blood. A knife was found hidden in the chimney.

It was Mann and his colleague, DC Riordan, who confronted Alcott on his return that evening. Mann addressed him thus:

'What's your name?'

'Alcott.'

'You know why we are here – we are police officers.'

'Yes, I know. I expected you, I thought there was something wrong when I returned home.'

Alcott was arrested, handcuffed and was told he was being detained on suspicion of murdering Dean. He was cautioned and then searched. A roll of bank notes and some coins, amounting to £11 4s 6d were found in his trouser pockets. Alcott explained, 'That's some of the money.' He then volunteered further information about himself:

> You know about my previous trouble, don't you? I did a murder
> in Germany and was reprieved by the King. Since then I have
> been worried about it.

It transpired indeed that Alcott had been sentenced to death on a previous occasion. When he was doing his National Service in the Grenadier Guards in Germany, he had deserted. In September 1948, he and a Sudeten Czech had beaten a German caretaker, Peter Helm, to death, in Montabaur. A court martial found Alcott guilty of murder on 4 January 1949. The sentence was not confirmed and so he was reprieved and then discharged.

The wider police investigation found other clues. A mackintosh and three empty cash bags were found in a garden in a house in Victoria Road. Joan Quinn of Upper Waybourne Lane, Farnham, recalled selling a knife on 18 August, but could not recall to whom she sold it. Bus staff were quizzed about any passengers they took from about 9–10 on the previous night. Old trousers were later found on Gun Hill.

Mant conducted a post mortem examination at Farnham Mortuary on the afternoon after the murder. He concluded, 'The cause of death had been multiple stab wounds of the chest. There were 20 stab wounds.' Two had penetrated the heart and seven the lungs. They had been 'delivered with great violence'. Death had occurred between about 8 and 11 pm. However, we know from other witnesses that it cannot have occurred after 9 pm, nor much before that hour.

On the night of 23 August, Alcott found himself in Aldershot police station. Superintendent Roberts was on hand to question him. Alcott was all too ready to talk about what he had done. He said he had been in Hampshire for three days and told them he had thrown his knife away. He added, 'It was obvious you would get me. We had quite a struggle and I left my fingerprints on the desk, I was going to France on holiday, I didn't really want the money, I had my own money.' He then began at the beginning. His holidays had begun on Monday 18 August. He had collected his wages from the Hither Green depot in South-East London.

Then he had taken a train to Farnborough to see the masters at his old school. On that night he stayed at the Commercial Hotel, Aldershot. On Tuesday and Wednesday nights he stayed at a shelter at Clapham South, before returning to The Commercial on Thursday night. He had spent each day in Aldershot and Farnborough, calling at Ash Vale for news of Turner, as has been related, though the man had actually been injured by Alcott, accidentally.

The climax came on the Friday night. Alcott explained it thus:

On the Friday night the 22nd August, having had no definite news as to Turner's condition, I kept thinking about his injuries. I was talking and joking with the booking clerk who I know as Dixie [Dean]. Dixie had some trouble with his books and his cash which was about £10 over. I had a sheath knife in the back pocket of my trousers. As I was talking to Dixie, I again visualised the injuries of fitter Turner. As from then I took out my knife from my pocket and attacked Dixie by stabbing him. He struggled and kicked at me and shouted for Paddy the porter, but I just stabbed him one after another. He stopped kicking at me and just slumped down.

Whilst Dean was dying, Alcott picked up the money and put it either into his pockets or into the cash bags in the mackintosh behind the door. He then picked up his knife, left the office, slammed the door and ran down the steps and out by the main entrance. He crossed the road and washed his hands in a stream. Alcott took a bus to Aldershot. There he dropped the cash bags and the mackintosh into a back garden. The rest is already known to the reader.

Alcott was formally charged at the magistrates' Occasional Court at Farnham on 25 August and was remanded in custody for a week.

Dean's funeral took place on the afternoon of 29 August. Mr Cook, chairman of the parish council, began a fund for Dean's widow. In addition to this, at least she was able to inherit £685 15s 11d, which her thrifty husband had been able to save during his short life.

Alcott was tried at the Surrey Assizes on 18 November, held at Kingston upon Thames. His defence put forward a plea of insanity, but this was rejected. He was found guilty and was sentenced to hang. There was an appeal, based on the fact that the jury had not been offered the verdict, 'Guilty, but insane'. However, on 17 December this was turned down, the Lord Chief Justice stating, 'I dare say the appellant is abnormal . . . but there is not the least ground for saying that there is any issue of insanity'. Alcott was duly hanged on 2 January 1952.

It is uncertain why Alcott killed Dean. Presumably it was due to his need for money, but this was never stated definitively. Alcott was clearly a very dangerous young man, having killed already in Germany and unfortunately having been discharged. At least he was not given another chance to do so.

17

The Difficult Passenger's End, 1962

'I stood up and pointed the gun at him, thinking he would realize it was a gun and be frightened.'

Travelling by train usually means spending time with people one would not normally be with, and from whom, for a temporary period, there is no escape. Fellow passengers can be, and often are, annoying. Those listening to ipods and other noisy devices, and of course, those using mobile phones, can be highly irritating. Occasionally a fellow passenger may remonstrate with them, but mostly the response is to seethe in silence. It is certainly rare that the annoying passenger is killed. But that is exactly what happened on a train in September 1962.

The Glasgow to London express left the Scottish city at 10.25 pm as usual. It was 29 September 1962. In the fourth compartment from the front of the train were Miss Helen Lewis, aged 23, of Bermondsey, her sister-in-law, Mrs Eileen Lewis, and David Anthony McKay, a thermal engineer of Altmore Avenue, East Ham, who was aged 28. McKay had politely asked if he could share the compartment with them. At Kilmarnock they were joined by Mr Francis Lennon, a 53-year-old train examiner, and Katherine, his wife, aged 42. These two lived at Kerrimuir Avenue, Hurlsford, Ayrshire. They all settled down quietly to get what rest they could. That peace was to be rudely interrupted.

The train was approaching Carlisle. It was then that Thomas McBain, a 20-year-old rock 'n' roll singer (known as 'Big Tom'), entered He was an apprentice engineer from Glendevo Square, Ruchazie, Glasgow. He was carrying a bottle of wine, some glasses and some cans of beer. McBain took a vacant seat. It was soon obvious that he had already been drinking. He acted in an uncouth manner. When the train was between Carlisle and Penrith, near Wreay, McKay and McBain began to quarrel. The argument turned violent as both young men rose to their feet. Two shots rang out. Confusion reigned. Meanwhile the communication cord was pulled in the next compartment. It was 2 am.

Dr John Laing of Aberdeen was in the next compartment and came next door. He saw what had resulted and wondered whether a knife or a gun had been used. McKay gave him a version of events. He admitted to shooting McBain, and then said that he had thrown the revolver out of the window. The gun, he said, he had taken from McBain's pockets. He later recalled that McKay had blood on his face and on his shirt; whilst McBain was lying, groaning, on the floor. Laing was with McBain when he died, but he did not tell McKay this news until later and McKay resented being kept in the dark about this.

The train stopped at Wreay and then carried on its journey to Penrith, where it halted. The carriage on which the shooting took place was uncoupled and put into a siding under police guard. Everyone on the train had their names and addresses taken. Thirty-six people, including a young honeymoon couple, were questioned. The train was only allowed to carry on with its journey to London at 6.40 am.

McKay was arrested at 3.45 am and told the police, 'I did not mean to shoot the bloke.' He was brought before a special court hearing at Mansion House, Penrith, on the day of the shooting. He was charged with murder. It all lasted only 90 seconds and he was then remanded in custody. He kept being thus remanded on another five occasions, each for a week. John Joseph McBain, the victim's brother, was found and he came down to identify the corpse. A post mortem indicated that his brother died of a haemorrhage and shock at having two bullets fired into him; one to the chest and one to the abdomen. Either one would have killed him. The gun was also found near to the railway line; it was a small automatic .25 Browning pistol.

There was an initial hearing at a magistrates' court on 1 November. Mr Guthrie Jones, defending McKay, saw the question of the ownership of the revolver as important. McKay insisted the gun had belonged to McBain and he said:

> I saw the gun in his pocket and I managed to get hold of it. In the struggle it went off. I dropped it out of the window because he kept coming for me . . . I told him 'I've got what you think you have got'. He turned to me on the seat so I jumped to my feet and took the gun out of my waistband and pointed it

towards him. He was still sitting down. He made as if to make a swipe and my gun went off. I don't know if it hit him. He went forward on the seat and then back. He was groaning. I said 'I think I had better get out of here'. He got up on his feet. I still had the gun in my hand and was trying to put my jacket on with the other hand. He tried to jump me. As he closed with me I pressed the trigger again. I had just about forgotten I had it in my hand. I fell onto the seat where the girls had been and he came down on top of me. I managed to stretch my hand up and threw the gun out of the ventilation window.

Yet it seems that McBain could not have been the possessor of a gun. His trouser pockets had large holes in them and a small pistol like the Browning would have fallen through them. Furthermore, a Mr Walker in Glasgow recalled being told there by McKay that he had a gun. McKay's story was thus a pack of lies.

The case came before the Cumberland Assizes at Carlisle on 15 January 1963. McKay pleaded not guilty to murder. Many more details emerged about what happened that night and also about the principal participants. First, McBain, 'Big Tom' as he was known to his intimates, had been drinking at the Tavern Bar, Glasgow, prior to boarding the train. He had had the equivalent of seven pints or fourteen single whiskies. John McClure, the sleeping car attendant, saw McBain after the latter entered the train. He knew McBain and did not think he was drunk nor quarrelsome. However, this seems to have been incorrect, according to other witnesses. Perhaps McBain had a few more drinks on the train itself.

The first compartment which McBain entered was the one occupied by Dr Laing among others. McBain also invited a friend into the compartment, too. Dr Laing commented, 'He was certainly drunk and a little belligerent and I said to someone in the compartment that I would not be surprised if we had some trouble from this fellow during the journey.' As the train travelled southward, McBain decided to go into the compartment next door.

He rattled on the door and saw there was a vacant seat. He took it. Mrs Lewis had been sleeping and she now awoke. McBain's eyes were half closed and his speech was slurred. He sat between McKay and Lennon; the three women were sitting opposite. McBain put his feet up on the seat opposite and asked Mrs Lennon if she minded. She said not. McKay, however, did, and told McBain that he did. McBain replied that he had paid his rail fare, so he was within his rights to put his feet where he liked. But he desisted shortly afterwards.

Once the train had passed Carlisle, Mrs Lewis reached for a cigarette. McBain put his feet on the seat opposite again. They hit her arm and dirtied her clothes whilst she was lighting up and she remonstrated with him, 'You should watch where you put your feet.' McKay spoke out against McBain, too, saying, 'You are not allowed to put your feet up there. After all, look what you did to the girl's cardigan.' McBain lit a cigarette, had second thoughts and flung it towards the ventilator. However, it bounced back and hit Mrs Lewis, who retorted, 'For crying out loud'. McBain apologised and said he hadn't meant to do it. Mrs Lewis accepted his apology and told him to forget it. 'I don't want to forget it' he replied. He asked the others why he couldn't put his feet up on the seat.

McKay rose to the challenge again, saying, 'You are not allowed, so let's forget it, and have a bit of peace and quiet.' McBain countered, 'You shut up or I'll make you get peace and quiet for the rest of the journey.' Both men were fully aroused to do battle. They stood up and squared off.

McKay then gave another version of events to that he had given previously:

> I got the impression that the other people in the compartment were scared of McBain and I thought I would have to persuade him to get out of the carriage to get some quiet. I stood up and pointed the gun at him, thinking he would realise it was a gun and be frightened. But he did not say anything and he was trying to hit the gun out of my hand. As he did so, I squeezed the gun to make sure if he did knock it, my hand would only swing away. I had no idea there was a shell in it. I was quite shocked.

Mrs Lewis then recalled, 'I saw McBain had staggered back to his seat. And McKay standing with a small gun in his hand.' At first she had thought that the small metallic object in McKay's had was a cigarette lighter. McBain clutched his side where he had been shot and lay back on his seat, smiling at McKay. Mrs Lewis fled the compartment. Miss Lewis pulled the communication cord in the next compartment. Mrs Lewis said that she had not seen the gun beforehand, thought that McBain was being objectionable and that McKay was being considerate in his behaviour hitherto.

Other facts emerged about McKay. He had had a previous conviction for possession of a firearm without a licence. In his flat was a small gun holster and various shooting magazines. There were a few spare bullets there and these exactly matched those which had been fired into McBain. There was no doubt that the gun used to kill McBain was McKay's.

Mr Cantley QC of the prosecution told him, 'You are entitled to take reasonable measures in your self defence, but not to shoot an unarmed man even if you think he might inflict some minor violence to you.' He then outlined the events of that fatal night. However, counsel for the defence said that McKay had been provoked and fired in self-defence. On the following day McKay was found guilty of manslaughter and was sentenced to four years in gaol. The interesting question to ask is why McKay was carrying a loaded gun in the first place. He had had no prior intention of shooting McBain, nor anyone else as far as is known. Clearly he had a fascination for firearms and this was to prove his undoing.

18

Throat Cutting on a Slow Train, 1964

'it was a very brutal murder, a completely motiveless attack
on this young girl for no reason'

Michael Szczup was 12 years old and a train spotter from Bracknell. He and three friends had spent Monday 29 June 1964 at Basingstoke station, noting down the trains which arrived at that busy station. Yet it is what happened afterwards that would prove more memorable. He later described the first stage of what should have been his return voyage:

We intended to return home by the 4.17 Basingstoke–Reading train. As soon as that train came in we got into the second class compartment in the first coach. Immediately the train left the station I went into the toilet compartment at the front end of the coach. When I opened the door of the toilet compartment I saw the legs of a lady on the floor. There was blood on the floor. I rushed into the coach and called out about what I had seen.

Paul Ramshir, a London chemist, had also seen what Szczup had and he had pulled the communication cord. Szczup jumped off the train, which had just left the station, and went to find a porter. After he had told him what had happened, he and his friends took the 4.37 train to Reading. The murder carriage was put into a siding.

The corpse was that of a teenage girl, dressed in her school uniform. Her throat was cut. Although at first it was wondered whether this was a case of suicide, such impressions were short-lived. PS Douglas Boekee was one of the first police officers on the scene and related:

There was a lot of blood on the floor which appeared to come from a severe wound in the throat. Her dress and jacket did not seem to be disturbed but I later saw that her stockings were badly laddered.

There were a number of clues in the compartment. There were pieces of broken glass near the body. Although fully clothed, the victim's shoes and beret were missing. In the compartment itself was a torn envelope addressed to 'David Manders, C3'. The address was missing. Inside were torn pieces of a birthday card, with the following message, 'To David, with love from Barbara and John'. Behind a seat was a brown carrier bag. In this was a cucumber and lettuce roll and a partly eaten packet of crisps. There was also a paper wrapper of a loaf, 'Midland Maid Farmhouse Bread'. This was only made in the Midlands.

What were the events leading up to this dreadful event? It had begun at Southampton station at 3.25. Yvonne Laker, a 15-year-old schoolgirl, was dark haired and shy. Her parents lived in Singapore, where her father, Peter, was a sergeant in the RAF. She had just spent the weekend with her grandparents, Major and Mrs Cyril Laker, in Burton on Sea and was about to return to her convent school in Maidenhead. They had taken a photograph of her before seeing her off at the station, for her father's benefit. She sat in the second class compartment of the first of three coaches on the train. Major Laker recalled, 'I recall no one being in the compartment but her when the train pulled out.' It was an open Pullman carriage, that is to say, it was a carriage with seats, but without partitions and there was no access to any other carriage.

The first stop on the train's journey was at Eastleigh. It was here that Peter Barnes, a recent graduate, and two friends, got on the train. He remembered seeing her and recalled, 'As far as I know no one sat besides her during the journey nor did I hear anyone speaking to her.' The second was at Winchester at 3.58, where Barnes and his friends alighted. The next was at Micheldever at 4.08. Just before the next stop, the train slowed down considerably. Then Basingstoke was reached at 4.22 and by then the murder had been done.

Detective Chief Superintendent Walter Jones of the Hampshire CID was in charge of the murder hunt. He had 70 detectives from Hampshire and Berkshire under him. A large blue mobile police headquarters was set up outside Basingstoke station. He stated at a press conference on the Monday of the murder, 'This appears to be the work of a maniac. As far as I can ascertain it was a very brutal murder, a completely motiveless attack on this young girl for no reason. There is no question of sexual assault or theft.' The chief constable was afraid the killer would strike again and urged Jones, 'Find this killer – quickly'.

Jones made a start. Forty of the train's passengers were interviewed. Tracker dogs found Yvonne's brown shoes and beret near the track between Micheldever and Basingstoke. A few pieces of green glass – the same sort which had been found on the train – were also found. These were pieced together and were found to almost make up a complete bottle. It was a half-size Cuesta sherry bottle. Jones made appeals for anyone who had seen anything relevant to come forward. He tried to locate the David Manders whose name was on the torn envelope. He also thought the label on the bread packaging was important and said, 'We are making enquiries in the Midlands to try and trace its origin, but we would like any of the train's passengers who saw this bag or the man who carried it, to come forward.'

The corpse was identified officially by her grandparents and by her father who was flown home from Singapore. Dr Keith Simpson, a Home Office pathologist, concluded that death was due to 'haemorrhage and shock due to a cut throat'. There was bruising on her forehead, probably caused by her being hit with a bottle and knocked unconscious. It was thought that she had then been dragged to the toilet and then had her throat cut by the now broken bottle. Death had occurred at about 4 pm. Her funeral was on 8 July at the Roman Catholic church at New Milton.

Yet what appeared to be a major breakthrough came through quite an unexpected fashion. On 2 July, Derek Pye, a 27-year-old unemployed farm worker of Hyde Road, Long Sutton, and a married man with children, was arrested by PC Myhill at 8.30 pm in Farnham and he was taken to Aldershot police station. He was charged with stealing a car belonging to a Mr Moss earlier that day. He was due to appear at the magistrates' court, but before he did, on the following day, he spoke to PC Eggleton. He told him, 'I am worried, I was on the train where the girl was murdered. I saw a man drag her along the corridor to the toilet.' He added, 'That train murder, I think I know who did it. I was on the train.' He was asked why he had not come forward earlier, and replied, 'I read it happened in a crowded train. As there was only us there. I didn't think it could be the same one.'

This seemed to be very important news indeed. Pye was asked about his movements on the day of the murder. Pye had taken a bus to Basingstoke at 9.30. At 11 am he was in the Anchor Inn, looking for a solicitor, who he later found. Pye explained that at 1 pm he had taken the wrong train from Basingstoke – he wanted to go to Winchester, where he planned to visit the army recruitment centre, but had gone on the wrong train and arrived at Reading. So he went back to Basingstoke. Then he went to Winchester, arriving at about 3 pm, and then took the train to Basingstoke – the same train as Yvonne Laker was travelling on. He entered the same compartment as her, in fact. He said that there was another man there, too.

When the train stopped at Micheldever, Pye went to the toilet, he said, and on his return, when the train was on its way again, he reported:

> When I came out, the man was helping her up. Her head was hanging down. I asked what was wrong and he said she had been sick. He took her into the toilet and was in there two or three minutes. He came out and started looking out of the window. I asked him if she was alright and he said it was none of my business. I went to the other end of the carriage and saw glass on the seat. I thought this is dangerous if a kiddy got hold of it. I picked it up and threw it out of the window.

The man was 'about five feet eight inches, black hair, aged 30 to 32 with full face and very smart'. When the train had stopped, Pye alighted and took a train from Reading to Hook at 6 pm and then a taxi to Odiham, where he had left his bicycle and cycled home, arriving between 8.30 and 9 pm. A neighbour saw him at this time and thought Pye looked normal. He also had a drink at the Grapes in Basingstoke and bought a half bottle of Cuesta sherry there. On the Wednesday after the murder, Pye was having a drink in his local, the Railway Arms. The publican started talking about the killing and said how terrible it was. To this Pye merely replied, 'Yes', lowered his head and then left the pub.

The police investigated Pye's stories and found some inconsistencies. Although there was a train to Hook at 5.41, Pye did not take it, as he was seen by John Hogg, an old schoolfriend, at Reading station at 7.30 pm. No taxi driver at Hook recalled taking anyone to Odiham that night. There was also uncertainty when Pye bought the half bottle of sherry for 10s; he claimed it was in the evening, but the licensee thought it was at 1 pm. And sherry bottles were found at his home. But Pye denied he had anything to do with the crime, stating, 'I never touched the girl. I had nothing at all to do with this thing.' Margaret Perira, a science officer at the Police Laboratory, examined his clothes, and though some blood was found on his shoes, this was his own.

Yet the police thought Pye was guilty. He was remanded in custody on several occasions, before finally being brought to trial at the Hampshire Assizes in Winchester on 26 November. Pye pleaded not guilty to the accusation of murder. His barrister argued that it was the other man in the train who committed the murder. The prosecution argued that this man did not exist and was merely a fiction. They said that the idea of someone committing a murder just yards from another man, albeit killing the girl in a toilet, was simply absurd. They also pointed to the pieces of broken glass in Pye's pocket, and alleged he bought the sherry bottle in the pub at 1 pm. Although they could not supply a motive for the murder, this was not required of them.

Yet a man had been seen leaving the train just before it stopped at Basingstoke station. It was slowing down and so it would certainly have been possible for someone to leave the train then. Railway workers saw a man acting suspiciously and seeming disconcerted when he saw them. He went in the direction of Winchester, and then turned north, running. Mrs Janet Agnell, working at a nearby factory, also saw this man. Finally, Ronald Bridges, a tractor driver, who was working nearby, stated, 'I started cutting the field about 4pm. About 4.30 pm I saw a man. He was walking up the side of the field from the direction of the railway line.' So perhaps Pye's story was true, after all. Yet we cannot be certain that this man was the killer. He may have been leaving the train for another reason, though if so it was certainly a coincidence. It was further noted that the glass in Pye's pocket did not have any traces of the victim's clothing on it.

This was not an easy case. The judge gave the jury a summary and then added:

> It is the sort of thing which makes one's blood boil to think that in the year 1964 there is or was on 29th June any man capable of such a foul deed . . . It is quite improper and quite the wrong approach for you to say 'Well, here is a ghastly crime, somebody's got to suffer'.

The jury took six and a half hours to reach their conclusion. They decided that Pye was not guilty. However, Pye could not leave as a free man because he was accused of lesser crimes. In the following year he was given an 18-month sentence for arson attacks in 1962–3.

The question remains as to who the mysterious stranger was who killed Yvonne and why he should do so. He presumably boarded to same compartment as her at Winchester, as did Pye. Waiting until his fellow male passenger was out of the way, he struck the poor girl over the head and when Pye returned, took her into the toilet and there cut her throat, throwing her beret and shoes out of the window, though we do not know why he did this. Presumably he must have had some form of mental kink to have killed for no apparent reason. It was certainly a dangerous act, with Pye so near at hand, but he managed to escape unscathed and unsuspected. Pye was obviously not very quick-witted and so the man was able to do what he did and evade justice.

19

Death of a Housewife, 1965

'I haven't the guts to kill a cat.'

Ash Vale railway station has had more than its fair share of murders associated with it. Two to be precise. It says much about the lack of historical knowledge, or memory, for when this second murder occurred, the local paper chose not to recall the earlier one, which has been chronicled in this book in Chapter 16. Oddly enough, they were only thirteen years apart.

Mrs Enid May Wheeler was the most ordinary of women. She had been married to her husband, Derek Francis Wheeler, a maker of electrical equipment, since 1955. They lived in a bungalow at Fireacre Road, Ash Vale, since 1959. There were no children. She had once worked at a factory at Ash Vale, but in the third week of March 1965, she had taken a job at Boots the chemists, in Wellington Street, Aldershot. She was clerk to the manager, Mr Burridge. He described her thus, 'a quiet, efficient sort of girl . . . I was very pleased to have her working for me.' It was a part-time job and she only worked in the mornings, taking a train home at lunch time. It was early closing day. Husband and wife usually said their goodbyes between 8.15 and 8.30 in the mornings. All very ordinary.

Yet her journey from Aldershot on Wednesday 7 April 1965 was to be different. She boarded the 12.24, in order to be home for lunch. This train had previously stopped at Guildford and was to travel on to Camberley, Staines and Waterloo. The journey from Aldershot to Ash Vale was only three miles and took about five minutes, the train travelling at 50 mph. It even passed Mrs Wheeler's home. However, when the train arrived at Ash Vale, one Patrick John Jenner alighted. Mrs Wheeler did not. He was 21 years old and was an unemployed labourer of Downshill Cottage, Runfold. He had lived in the district for all his young life.

Jenner told the porter there that he had seen a man, whom he had only caught a glimpse of and could not recognize or describe, and a woman together on the train. He was very agitated. His name and address were taken for further reference. Ivor Lawes, another member of rail staff, had noticed that one of the carriage doors was open before the train's arrival at the station. But no one got out and there was no one in the compartment. Although there was no sign of any blood, some of the seats there had been slashed. Furthermore, there was, however, a bag, an umbrella and a parcel of towels there, with no apparent owner. Where was their owner?

Richard Powell, the stationmaster, was trained in first aid. He wondered if there had been an accident. So he and two colleagues took the first aid kit and walked by the line from Ash Vale station. They found Mrs Wheeler, lying near the track and stained with blood from several wounds. Powell tried mouth-to-mouth resuscitation, but without any success.

The still breathing body was taken by train to Aldershot and then conveyed to the Cambridge Military Hospital, where she was dead on arrival. Major Kenneth Ellis certified this. Her husband formally identified her at 5 pm. The post mortem was carried out by Dr Keith Mant, a Home Office pathologist. He found 17 stab wounds on the body, some of which had penetrated the lungs and heart. Her hands had been injured, indicative of the fact that she had tried to defend herself from attack. There were also other injuries which were consistent with the woman being thrown from the train. He thought her neck had been gripped for a short time. There was no evidence of any sexual interference. This was now a murder investigation and Detective Chief Superintendent Walter Jones of Hampshire CID was in charge. He was soon replaced by Detective Superintendent John Place of the Surrey CID, but men from the two forces worked together on the case. Two other officers saw the corpse in the mortuary that evening; Detective Chief Inspector Owen Breach and Detective Inspector Gibbs.

Meanwhile, Jenner proceeded on his journey to Frimley. He spent the trip in the same compartment as Mary Broad, a housewife, who worked part-time in Farnborough. For a minute he sat opposite her and said nothing. Then he asked her to light his cigarette. She did not smoke and said so. Then he told her that he had seen a man and a woman alone in the train a few minutes previously, and that he was going to the Southern Counties Car Auction in Frimley that afternoon. Arriving at the station, which was also her destination, he opened the door for her and then fell out, putting his hands in front of his body to stop himself.

At first, Jenner followed Mrs Broad, but she redirected him in the correct route to the motor show. Presumably he never went there, because at 12.45, Anthony Grant, conductor on a bus from Camberley, took his fare from Frimley to Aldershot. There, he went to the police station and asked if there was any news about what had happened on the railway that afternoon. At first, the police there saw him as a potential witness. Perceptions were to change that night.

Jenner was there for a considerable period of time. At 11.10 pm, Breach and Gibbs went to see him. Breach began to talk to Jenner:

> I told him that the body had been found on the railway line between Aldershot and Ash Vale, and it appeared she has been stabbed to death in a railway carriage . . . I told him that it was believed he could help us with inquiries into her death because he had travelled in the carriage which Mrs Wheeler had also travelled. 'Oh God! Is she dead?' I asked him if he could throw any light upon her death. 'Not me. I haven't the guts to kill a cat'.

Breach was unhappy with how truthful Jenner was being and told him that further enquiries were under way, but the latter persisted in denials, 'Well, I didn't kill her.' He was charged and then given a caution. Jenner refused to say any more, 'Not until I have seen a solicitor and got legal aid.' Mr Stredder, a Farnham solicitor, agreed to represent him.

Jenner was charged with the murder on 8 April and was taken before the magistrates' court at Farnham fire station on the following day. The room used was small for the purpose and was filled with reporters. Jenner was 'a smallish figure with short dark hair'.

Meanwhile, the police had investigated the land near the railway track between Aldershot and Ash Vale, as well as the railway carriage where it was assumed Mrs Wheeler had been attacked. Taken together, it was pretty damning. There was a tie clip and an ignition key near the corpse. Neither belonged to Mrs Wheeler, but a tie clip of the same kind had been given to Jenner as a present in the previous year. A white-handled sheath knife and sheath was also found nearby. It was 24 feet from the line and could easily have been thrown out of the train window. Jenner was known to possess such knives and had been seen with one on the previous day. James Newbury, Jenner's ex-boss, and John Barker, Jenner's brother-in-law, identified it as being very much like the one in Jenner's possession. He claimed he had lost one sometime before and another had been thrown in a specified rubbish tip recently. On investigation, the latter could not be found. Jenner said that his interest in knives was restricted to throwing them at trees. In the carriage, on the door which had been swinging loose, was a palm print and a fingerprint. There was blood on Jenner's shoes and jacket. It was type AMW. Jenner's blood group was O. Mrs Wheeler's was A. Finally, Jenner's hands were cut. He tried to explain this by his fall from the train to the platform at Frimley, but evidence was given that the platform was smooth, so that this would have been impossible.

The railway staff were interviewed by the police. Although Eric Cottam, who had been manning the signal box, had not seen anything unusual, one of his colleagues was more helpful. Ivor Lawes, waiting on the Ash Vale platform, had been able to see both sides of the train as it pulled into the station, so could see the open door. He recalled Jenner appearing agitated and nervous. Yet Edward Chater, a junior porter and an acquaintance of Jenner's, talked to him and thought he was 'perfectly normal'. Jones, the guard, had inspected the train at Guilford and had not seen anything out of the usual there.

At the magistrates' court, a little more was learnt about Jenner's movements up to the time of the murder. On the Saturday beforehand, he and Alec Kellett, a porter at Ash Vale, went to London by train, returning on the following day. Kellett recalled Jenner wearing a tie clip. They had been 'stung' in the capital. Jenner told his friend that on their next trip there, he would take his sheath knife with him and he showed Kellett the weapon when they returned home. Kellett assumed this was merely a jest.

On the Wednesday morning of the murder, Kellett and Jenner drove around Aldershot in the former's car. Jenner talked about attending the car auction later that day. Kellett dropped Jenner off at Aldershot station. Jenner wondered whether he should take the bus from Aldershot to Frimley or the train. Because the train was arriving first, he boarded that and shared a compartment with Mrs Wheeler. The rest we can surmise. Jenner attacked Mrs Wheeler, then opened the door and threw her and the knife out of the train.

Although he pleaded not guilty at the Surrey Assizes held at Kingston on 8 July 1965, Jenner was found guilty after the jury had 28 minutes of discussion. He was sentenced to life imprisonment. In an earlier decade he would have been hung. It is unclear what his motive was. However, he was known to be an enthusiast about knives and clearly this had much to do with what he did. Mrs Wheeler was very unlucky to have been in the same compartment as him on that day – had the bus to Frimley had been scheduled to arrive before the train, Jenner would have boarded that and her life would have been saved. Unfortunately, this was not the case.

20

Killed for a Snub, 1965

'if she had not led me on I would never have got into
the situation which I did'

Patricia Grace Woolard's life had been a mixed one, but it seemed to be
looking up in the 1960s. She had been born on 19 February 1934 at
Ramsgate. Her father, Leslie Ward, was employed in the railways and was
a keen trade unionist. His daughter attended Barnehurst Primary School
at Derby Heath, when the family lived at Barnehurst. Clearly a bright
girl, she passed her 11 plus exam and went to Dartford Grammar School,
where she did well, but declined a place at university. She had a number
of jobs on leaving school aged 17. These included working as a bank
clerk, at a TV firm in Erith and as a clerk at a plywood manufacturers.
However, she fell in love with an older man whom she met when she
accompanied her father to a trade union conference. This was Alfred
Britten (born in 1924), a railway clerk. They married in 1953 and lived in
Edendale, Bognor. The marriage, which was childless, fell into
difficulties due to a perceived lack of compatibility. Her husband agreed
to a divorce and consented to be the guilty party. They divorced in 1961
and she changed her surname by deed poll to her mother's maiden name.
She returned to live with her parents at South Road, Whitstable, Kent.

From 1961 to 1963, she worked as a clerk and an educational assistant.
In 1963 she began as a pupil teacher for Kent County Council. She
started a residential teacher training course at Bognor, specializing in
divinity, art and craft. She was a talented potter and made a number of
figures, some of which were displayed by the college in exhibitions. She
had completed her teacher training course in July 1965. Her interest in
pottery, inadvertently, was a factor in her eventual death. She had left
some of her work at the college. These were a series of figurines
representing characters from *The Canterbury Tales*. With an eye to selling

these to a boutique in Canterbury, on 3 September, she went down to the college to see Mary Gale, assistant librarian at the college library, who had been keeping her work for her. She took the 8.40 train from Whitstable to Victoria, and then changed for Bognor, arriving at 12.20. Her father later said, 'Patricia was not afraid of travelling alone, and I would think on the train journey she would try to avoid conversation by reading. She very rarely went out and so far as I know did not have any male friends.' She had lunch alone. Then she met Mrs Gale, and Charles Woollaston, an art and crafts lecturer, when she collected her pottery figures, putting them into a raffia bag, and paid off a few debts. Then Patricia caught the 3.30 bus for the railway station.

Although she had hoped to take the 4 pm fast train to Gatwick, she just missed it. Instead, she took the stopping service to Victoria. This left at 4.06 pm. It was a three-unit electric car, with two carriages to each unit. Frederick Horton, a ticket collector, recalled her boarding it and sitting in a compartment in the first carriage behind the engine. Once ensconced in the compartment she sat with her back to the engine and began to read. At 4.30, the train stopped at Littlehampton and Albert Isaac, the new driver, saw her there. The next stop was Horsham and Mary Bishop recalled seeing her alone there at 5.07 pm. The train left at 5.12.

So far, her journey had been entirely predictable and ordinary. Mary Bishop sat in the compartment behind Patricia's. She later recalled, 'During the journey, my attention was drawn to something happening on the train. I heard a muffled scream and a thud carry from behind where I was sitting.'

At 5.33, and after several more stops, the train was at platform 2 of Gatwick Airport station. Frederick Manwell, motorman, got out of the train and saw that all was not well. Along with Joseph Quigley, a porter, they entered Patricia's compartment. They could see her lying there, but did not suspect what had really happened at first. Manwell later explained, 'I went across to give assistance and I lifted her and then discovered blood under her head. She was lying on the same side of the coach as the girl had been sitting that I saw at Horsham'. He called the station foreman and Quigley stood by the compartment door as all the train's passengers were required to leave the unit, which was shunted away, and they were asked to board the rest of the train, which proceeded to Victoria. The police and a doctor were called.

That evening, Leslie Ward had the unenviable task of officially identifying his daughter's corpse at Redhill Hospital. It was not a pleasant sight. Dr Basil Raeburn made out the death certificate. On the following day, Dr Arthur Mark, a Harley Street pathologist, examined the body and found bruises and a number of stab wounds, one to the neck and others to the left side of the chest. One of the latter had been fatal, having pierced a lung and then the heart. There was also a wound to the back of the left hand, probably where the victim had tried to defend herself. All these injuries had been caused by a knife and they had not been self-inflicted.

Patricia's belongings were found scattered over the next few days. PC John Bevan found a lady's leather purse at the Three Bridges railway station at 8.45. John Davey, a schoolboy, found a handbag in River Mole Wood, not far away. Timothy Maslem found Patricia's medical card a mile from the same station. It was presumed that the killer left the train at this station, which is between Horsham and Gatwick.

Yet there were few clues to the killer's identity. No one saw anyone leave or enter the compartment. Although there was plenty of bloodstains, the only fingerprints were those of the victim. Nor could any weapon be located at the scene. The motive was obscure, too, because no one was known to have a grudge against Patricia. Her former husband was safely accounted for, and in any case, the divorce had been reasonably amicable and they had not seen each other since. Although the victim's clothes had been disarranged and her knickers had been tugged at, there was no sign of any sexual interference or attempt at the same. She did not have much money on her – perhaps about £2 at the most. His identity was obscure. A nurse did see a man later that evening (at about 6.30 pm) at Brighton station with a bandaged hand, but this man could not be traced. Another witness, Ernest Tallintyre, saw a man with light brown hair in the same compartment as the victim, but could provide no further information.

Detective Superintendent John Place was put in charge of the case. He appealed to anyone who had been at Three Bridges station that evening to come forward with any relevant information. WPS Pamela Lopez was dressed as Miss Woolard on 7 September and took the same route in order to try and jog people's memories. An identikit picture of the wanted man, based on the description of the man with the bandaged hand at Brighton, was shown on television on the following day. There were 80 reports of sightings of such a man. In the next few months, police spoke to 15,000 people.

Mrs Gale was questioned. She said that Patricia 'did not mention any other person, either that she was going to meet, or whom she had seen. Miss Woolard never mentioned any men friends.' She added, 'She was looking particularly attractive and seemed very happy.' Her husband was also questioned. He said, 'Patricia was generally a clean living girl, both physically and morally and was fairly reserved, and in my opinion, is not the sort of girl who would invite the attention of men friends.'

Earlier that evening, in a house on Clymping Road, Ifield, Sussex, between 5.50 and 5.55, one Michael Robert Stephen Gills, a 32-year-old labourer, arrived home. Roger Boseley-Yemm, who was engaged to his step-daughter, was in the house and recalled, 'I noticed he had a spot of blood on his vest. He put the shirt to soak in water, and I knew he washed his vest.' He said he felt unwell. On the following day, the two men read about the murder in their morning newspaper. Yemm said that Gill did not talk about it.

Next day, Detective Inspector Basil Morris called at the house. He wanted to talk to Gills. Why was this? It was not that there was any evidence to link Gills, or indeed, anyone, to the crime. However, Gills was a known criminal and it is routine police work to check up on anyone of this type in the locality of a major crime (Ifield is only a bus ride away from the Three Bridges station, where the killer presumably alighted).

Gills's background was not a happy one. Born in Poplar on 27 October 1933, he had got on well with his father, a docker and once regular soldier. But his father died when he was 6 and his mother remarried within a year. Gills suffered from nightmares, nail biting and bed wetting. Relations between mother and son were poor. Evacuation to Banbury in 1939 proved traumatic for the young lad and he turned to petty crime, stealing a bicycle when he was 10. From then on, his life was one of crime, imprisonment (eight short terms from six months to two years) and short spells of employment. Most of his crimes were theft and burglary. However, a spell in Borstal showed that he was not averse to threatening others with a knife. He was deemed hardworking, but moody, with a violent temper and capable of injuring anyone who obstructed him. His jobs included a spell in the Royal Artillery from 1951 to 1954, but he was discharged in Egypt for lack of discipline and was uninterested in military matters. He also worked in mills and factories, as a porter, labourer, lorry driver and machine operator, but his time keeping was poor and gaol sentences tended to terminate his legitimate employment.

Gills's relations with women were mixed. He was very bitter towards his mother, who, he claimed, had disowned him at 13. However, he married one Catherine Amelia in October 1962, and he treated her like a surrogate mother (she was ten years his senior). He lived with her and her daughter, Elaine Brooke. Their life seemed normal enough and in 1965 she was pregnant.

From 1963, his crimes changed in character. Hitherto they had not been against the person. Now he began to assault women. One attack was on Jean Plaisted at Bognor on 14 July 1965; she had been pushed to the ground and threatened with a knife. The attacker ran off in the direction of the caravan park (Gills and family were holidaying there). Indeed, when the police questioned him in September 1965, he was actually on bail pending a court hearing for an assault on a woman at Crawley (and had in fact only been released from prison in July 1965). His probation officer referred to him as 'basically an inadequate and immature person, strongly dependent on support and approval'. Dr Neustatter labelled him 'an aggressive psychopath with paranoid tendencies'. He had also changed in outward behaviour – up to 1963 he was swaggering and aggressive, afterwards he was nervous and quiet in appearance.

It was alleged that Gills was not at work on the day of the murder, but he denied this. He said, 'I was there. I was at the back of the works all the time because I didn't feel well.' He also said he had injured his hand that day at work, but there was no evidence that that had happened there. The police also saw him later that month. They tried to ascertain his movements on the day of the murder. It soon emerged that, despite his vagueness and prevarications, he had not been at work that afternoon. Gills tried to pretend he had been in the paint room, hence no one seeing him. Yet the room was locked and a colleague said, 'There is over £1000 worth of paint in here. I keep it locked all the time except when I was in there.' A policeman concluded, 'I understand now that you say you were not at work after all, but went down to Brighton station.'

Apparently he had caught a train to Brighton in order to see the film, *Fanny Hill*. Unable to view it, because it would mean returning home late and his wife would worry, he walked around town and had some cups of tea. Returning to the station, he met an old work friend of his, an Italian whom he called 'Poppa', and whose real name was Orlando Lazzaro. The two men lived near to one another and so they caught a train just before 4 pm from Brighton and later changed at Three Bridges for Crawley. The two then parted and Gills took a bus home. The police searched his home, but could find nothing incriminating, and had his clothes sent to the police laboratory. Nothing conclusive could be found. There was no evidence he was ever on the same train as Patricia, as no one saw him either enter or leave. There was certainly nothing that they could charge him with this time. In any case, he was soon found guilty of the Bognor assault and given two years in gaol.

The inquest was held at Reigate on 14 January 1966. The verdict was murder by person or persons unknown. It looked as if this would be another unsolved murder.

However, in June 1966, events took a dramatic turn. Gills contacted the investigating officers and asked that they visit him. They did on 6 June and he told them what had happened. Gills explained that he had left work on 3 September at 12.45, collecting his wages as he did so. He had taken a bus to Crawley and then a train to Brighton as already stated. Whilst there, he purchased a sheath knife with a six inch blade, 'because I intended to use it on a bloke whom I had some trouble with whilst in Wandsworth'. After having missed the film at the Continental as already mentioned, he went back to the railway station. He met his Italian acquaintance and they caught the 3.58 train from Brighton. They changed at Crawley station and took a train to Three Bridges, where both alighted (at 4.38), but instead of going home from there, Gills went to the other platform and took a train (at 4.42) back to Horsham, arriving there at 4.56. He then waited for the train to Victoria.

When the train arrived, he went along the platform, looking into the compartments. He caught a glimpse of Patricia. According to him:

> In there was a young woman. She was sitting by a big basket, in the corner near the door. I sat in the corner on the opposite side. She was wearing a white coat, a dress, the colour of which I can't remember. She was aged about 26–30 years and attractive looking. She also had with her an off white attaché case and a handbag. During the journey she was reading a book. Whilst reading it, she kept looking up now and again and it seemed like she was looking at me. It seemed that I was onto a good thing, so I then moved up the seat and sat opposite her. Nothing was said until we got to Faygate, when I asked her 'What about it?' at which she sort of snubbed me, and turned her nose up in the air. All along she had been showing plenty of leg, and did not bother to cover them up. At this I got annoyed because in my earlier life

I had been, at 13 years old, disowned by my own mother, and had been snubbed and not treated fairly by other women. They had treated me as though I had something wrong with me, or that I was a 'leper'. And all the bitter hate and resentment that I had for women came to a head. Then I asked her something again, the exact words I cannot remember. She put the book down, looked straight at me and answered back. Here again, I cannot remember what was said, but I know it was not a very nice reply. At this I stood up in front of her. She said, 'Go away. Leave me alone or I will pull the cord and report you to the police.' I then grabbed hold of her to stop her pulling the cord. We struggled for a short while, at which she gave a short scream. I then pulled out the knife and stabbed her twice on the left side. Where exactly I do not know as she was twisting and turning. She was then sitting down when this happened. She screamed again. A lot louder this time. I know that at this point I had gone past the point of no return. I do not remember what happened between this and stabbing her in the throat. She fell to the floor, I tried to push her under the seat.

Gills then got off at the next station, the Three Bridges (at about 5.30), taking her handbag and the attaché case. He washed himself at the toilet at the station platform. He hid the purse there and then, on leaving, threw the case and the handbag into the stream. He caught a bus to Langley Green and went home; the newspaper in which he had wrapped the knife was left on the bus. He hid the knife among old paintbrushes at home. Eventually he broke up the knife and hid its parts in bushes not far from his home.

He concluded his statement thus:

I know it is rather late to say I am sorry, but I never had any intention in the first place of committing this crime. Whilst this is a serious crime, things did get out of my control. For which I am heartily and truly sorry for I am not trying to put all the blame on the woman, but if she had not led me on I would never have got into the situation which I did. I would like to say once again that I am very sorry for. Especially to her parents.

There was some question as to what he thought about women in general.

Gills stated 'You know I have never had a fair deal from a woman except my wife. Even my own mother threw me out when I was only 13 and she didn't want to know me.' Chief Inspector Stothard asked him, 'Do you hate women?' Gills replied, 'I do them that snub me and stick their noses up in the air.' Stothard then asked, 'Did you travel on the train where the murder was committed?' Gills answered, 'You know I did.'

One possibility, of course, was that this confession was a tissue of lies, based on reading newspaper reports and with the intention of gaining a little cheap notoriety. Prisoners do make such false confessions. Yet the police did not think this was the case, for a number of reasons. First, an examination of bus and train times showed that Gills's journey as he described it was perfectly possible. Secondly, Gills stated that Patricia was reading a book, a fact not stated in the press. Thirdly his approach to Patricia was said to have occurred at Faygate and that agreed with Mrs Bishop's statement. Fourthly, Gills said he struck her on the hand, and that he stabbed her in the throat with a knife – the press did not mention the cut to the hand and had said that her throat had been cut. There were no inconsistencies in his story. Finally, the location of Patricia's belongings was where he stated.

There was some question over Gills's mental state. Dr Lotinya was senior medical officer at Wandsworth prison. He assessed Gills as 'emotionally an unstable person, abnormally impulsive and egocentric, who is unable to learn from experience and who, having failed to develop normal moral and social standards, cannot conform to accepted social usage'. He thought that Gills was fit to plead, but that his abnormal mind had substantially impaired his mental responsibility at the time of the offence. Gills was tried at the Surrey Assizes held at Kingston upon Thames on 27 October. He pleaded not guilty to murder, but guilty to manslaughter. Although cleared of murder, he was found guilty of manslaughter due to diminished responsibility. The judge admitted, 'your mind was greatly disturbed by mental troubles'. His sentence was 15 years, to run concurrently with his existing two–year sentence for assault.

Gills was an unpleasant character and it was Patricia's fatal misfortune to meet him – entirely by chance – on the Gatwick train. Once Gills was in the same compartment as her, or probably almost any young woman, the outcome was probably inevitable. Perhaps the only fortunate aspect to this case is that Gills confessed in the following year, because had he not done so, this murder would almost certainly have remained unsolved. If that had been the case, perhaps Gills would have killed again.

21

Other Railway Crimes, 1897–2008

The railway crimes already recounted are not the only ones in British crime history. There have been many more and it is impossible to cover them all in much details. Here is a synopsis of some of them.

The first female victim, 1897

Elizabeth Camp was aged 33, and planned to marry Edward Berry, a Walworth fruiterer. She worked in the Good Intent Tavern, on East Street, Walworth. She was deemed a reliable employee and seemed a very ordinary young woman. That is, until Thursday 1 February 1897.

She spent the afternoon of her day off in Hammersmith and then Hounslow, with her two married sisters. On entering a second class carriage at Hounslow station at 7.42 that evening, her sister warned her that 'the third class is safer for women'. Ignoring this well-meant advice, Elizabeth travelled on this stopping service to Waterloo, in order to meet her fiancé.

Unfortunately, when the train pulled into its destination at 8.25, she did not alight from it. Her corpse, with its head battered, was found in the carriage. The police soon found the weapon – a bloodstained pestle – which had been thrown out of the train between Putney and Wandsworth. The head porter at Putney recalled seeing a man in her carriage there. It was thought that she had been killed between these two stations.

It was unclear why she had been killed. She had spent the day shopping, but her purchases had all been sent on to her home. She had very little money on her. No one was known to have had a grudge against her. However, there were a number of suspects.

Berry himself had been waiting at Waterloo for her. Furthermore, he was with two other men for the hour previous to that. A former boyfriend, William Brown, was also ruled out, because he was at work in the Prince Albert that evening. Thomas Stone, a Hounslow resident and a friend of one of her sisters, and who had spent some time with both of them prior to Elizabeth's departure, came under suspicion, especially because he could not account for his movements for the remainder of the day. However, there was no proof against him, so he could not be detained.

Other witnesses spoke of seeing suspicious-looking men, some with bandaged hands, leaving the train that evening. One had gone for a drink in a nearby pub, but when found, it transpired that he had injured himself repairing a bicycle. One Mr Marshall, a young man from Reading, was also questioned. The police thought a wandering lunatic on Blackheath might be responsible. As late as 1906 a soldier confessed to the crime, but was found to be lying.

The train company offered a reward of £200 to anyone who could identify Elizabeth's killer. It was never claimed. Sir Melville Macnaghten, a senior police officer, offered the following judgement on the case:

> The murder of Miss Camp was wholly without motive, and was no doubt perpetrated by some homicidal maniac. Such men, I believe, have no recollection of their guilty acts, which pass out of their minds as soon as they have been committed.

Presumably the murder was an impulsive act, though clearly the killer had violence on his mind, for he was carrying a pestle on his person. But as to who and why, we are no wiser more than a century later and Elizabeth has the dubious distinction of being the first woman to have been killed on a train in Britain.

Underground murder, 1914

The Starchfields were a poor family. John Starchfield, the father, was popularly seen as a hero, having tackled an armed robber in 1912 and being wounded in the process. But in private he was a different man. He stole from his wife and had hit her. This helps account for the fact that he and his wife had separated, with Mrs Starchfield and their 5-year-old son, Willie, living in lodgings in Hampstead Road, whilst he sold newspapers and lived near Tottenham Court Road.

On Thursday 8 January, Willie was being looked after by a neighbour. Just after noon, he was sent out on an errand to a nearby shop. He never returned. Later that afternoon, at 4.30 pm on a third class Underground carriage, a terrible discovery was made. Willie had been strangled. This crime had taken place between Mildmay Park and Dalston Junction. He was probably taken to either Camden Town station or Chalk Farm station before entering the Underground. A post mortem examination revealed that the boy had been given a cake that afternoon, perhaps as a way of enticing him away.

Later, a cord was found and this was thought to have been the murder weapon. It was unknown as to why he had been killed, since robbery could not have been a motive. Nor had he been interfered with. Perhaps someone had a grudge against either or both of his parents. One theory was that the associates of the criminal whom John Starchfield had helped apprehend two years ago might have been responsible.

However, during the investigation, John Starchfield himself was identified as the killer. He lacked an alibi for the time of the murder and was seen by witnesses with his son that afternoon. Yet this identification was not confirmed by other witnesses, and under cross-examination, one witness was unable to properly identify Starchfield. Others came forward to say they had seen the doomed lad with a woman. Starchfield was dismissed as innocent. Chief Inspector Gough concluded, 'Neither Starchfield nor his wife bears a good character, but, so far as we have gone, there is no evidence to associate them in any way with the crime, and in fact, no witnesses of any importance have been traced.'

The boy's father died two years later. Curiously enough, a few weeks previously, a bottle had been found in the Thames, bearing a confession from him. Yet, the handwriting did not match his, and so it was deemed a hoax. John Fitzpatrick, a porter, also confessed to the murder, claiming his motive was robbery. Willie, though, had no money on him so Fitzpatrick was dismissed from enquiries.

It is impossible to know what really happened. Any man, woman or child could have taken the boy away to the Underground and either killed him on the platform or on an empty carriage. Why anyone would want to do so is unknown, and one policeman assumed it must have been the work of a homicidal maniac.

The Kidbrooke mystery, 1929

Mrs Winifred East and her husband parted on the morning of Wednesday 13 March 1929; he to his work and she to take trains to Bexleyheath to see an old friend of hers. Unbeknown to either, this was to be the last time they would see each other alive.

Mrs East spent a pleasant day with Mrs Margaret Richards. They said their goodbyes at Barnehurst station so Mrs East could catch the 7.43 train to London Bridge. From there, she would travel to Liverpool Street and meet her husband, before catching a train back home to Leytonstone. Mrs East sat alone in a third class compartment. Mrs Richards described what happened next:

> I stood at the carriage door talking just a moment with my arm across the entrance to the compartment, and as I stood there, I felt a slight touch on my arm. I immediately let my arm fall and a young man stepped into the compartment. He sat on the same seat as Mrs East, but he sat at the further end. The train started at once.

Mrs East never arrived home that night. It was the following day that a train driver saw her corpse. It was lying near the track between Kidbrooke and Eltham stations. She had been killed by being run over by a train after falling onto the line. Yet it was soon concluded that this was neither accident nor suicide, but murder. There were bruises on her body that would indicate that a struggle had occurred before she had been pushed from the train – or had jumped out in a desperate attempt at escape.

Mrs Richards could not give much help, except to say that the man she saw enter the compartment was aged between 20 and 30 and that he was slightly built and of medium height. He was wearing an overcoat and a cap. Other witnesses claimed to have heard noises in a compartment between Eltham and Kidbrooke. They thought the killer alighted at Kidbrooke, but in this they seem to have been mistaken.

It was presumed that the young man seen by Mrs Richards was the killer, but not necessarily so. He could have alighted before the train reached Eltham, allowing some other man to enter and kill Mrs East. Why anyone should want to molest her is another question. Was it an attempt at robbery or rape? Various candidates were suggested to the police over the next few years, but none was ever charged. The mystery remains to this day.

The death of a countess, 1957

It is rare for members of the aristocracy to be killed, despite what one may read in detective fiction. However, the 73-year-old Countess Teresa Lubienska, once possessed of landed estates in Poland, had fallen on hard times. She had survived the concentration camps and by 1947 was living in a small rented flat on Cromwell Road, London. Much of her time was spent lobbying to help former Polish prisoners of war and concentration camp survivors.

On the evening of 25 May 1957, she had been attending a birthday party of a fellow countrywoman of hers in a house in Florence Road, Ealing. She took a Piccadilly line train from Ealing Common and parted with her travelling companion, a priest, at Earl's Court tube station, while she rode on alone. She alighted at Gloucester Road station just after 10.19 pm.

What exactly happened next we do not know. But a member of Underground staff saw her staggering towards the lift. She had been stabbed. She said that she had been attacked by a bandit or bandits. Although taken to hospital as fast as possible, she died of her wounds that night. They were caused by a short-bladed knife or knives.

There was a very extensive police investigation. Thousands of people who lived in that part of London, tourists, known criminals and railway staff were interviewed. The police assumed that the killer must have stabbed her near the platform when the other alighting passengers had left there. He must then have run up the back stairs and so left the tube station that way. He could not have used the lift because that was manned and the attendant saw no one suspicious.

No one was ever convicted of the murder and the police never had any named suspect. One theory was that this was a political assassination, perhaps by a Soviet agent or by someone in the Polish organizations for whom she worked and was a traitor. This view is still held to this day by some Poles.

However, the reality is almost certainly far more prosaic. Countess Teresa was a fiery and outspoken individual. She had strong views on bad behaviour and foul language which were all too prevalent among the youth of London. And she was not afraid to make her views known and to reprimand youngsters in the street. This was not always a safe policy for an elderly and vulnerable old lady. Two witnesses told the police that they had seen a group of young men of the 'Teddy Boy' type in the vicinity of the tube station that evening. One group had been indulging in horseplay in the station itself; later a few youths had been seen running away from the murder scene. These lads were never identified, but it seems fair to surmise that the countess was caught up in an argument with them and one or more fatally attacked her with penknives.

The Great Train Robbery, 1963

It would be impossible to write about railway crime in Britain and omit any reference to perhaps the best known railway crime of all. This is so famous that it has been thought just to include a brief outline of events. As with its predecessor in 1855, it was well planned, competently executed and yet it ended with all the gang being apprehended. It was also the biggest value robbery in Britain until the Brinks Mat heist of 1983.

On 8 August 1963, the Glasgow to Euston travelling post office train was on its way south. It was composed of a diesel locomotive and twelve carriages and had run on this line since 1838. It was used as a mobile sorting office and also carried cash – the largest amounts being carried just after bank holidays. On board were almost £2.6 million worth of old notes ready to be delivered at the Bank of England for destruction. These were in the second carriage after the locomotive in the carriage known as the High Value Package Coach. The train was approaching Sears crossing near Ledburn, near Mentrose in Buckinghamshire. It was about 3 in the morning.

Jack Mills, the driver, saw the red signal on the lights ahead at the crossing and applied the brake. He told David Whitley, the locomotive's fireman, to get out and telephone the signalman. What neither of them knew was that the gang had tampered with the signals; by temporarily powering the red light and covering up the green one. Mills was hit on the head and fell down the railway embankment (he died in 1970, perhaps as a result of the injuries he then sustained); he then was forced to drive the train to Bridgeo railway bridge. Here the fifteen strong gang, wearing helmets and ski masks and armed with sticks and iron bars, overcame the four postal workers in the coach and loaded all the money from the train into their waiting lorry and fled to their headquarters.

This was a nearby farmhouse. They had intended to remain there for some time while the hue and cry died down. Yet, with the robbery being national news, £260,000 being offered in reward money and a team of crack detectives under Detective Chief Superintendent Thomas Butler and 'Slipper of the Yard' after them, they decided to split and run with the money. An anonymous tip off led the police to their hideout.

Although the thieves had departed, their traces were all too easy to find.

The gang had been led by a known armed burglar, Bruce Reynolds, who had recently been released from prison. He knew when the mail train would be carrying the maximum amount of money, and gathered together a number of other known criminals. Various schemes had been discussed before the one employed with such effectiveness.

As with their predecessors in 1855, they made their own blunders. Prior to the raid, the gang had drunk bottled beer and played Monopoly. The man left behind to clean up after them had not done a good job. Fingerprints were left all over their base. Another error was that the purchase of the farmhouse was made by a known associate of Reynolds and a bona-fide law firm was used in the arrangement. Furthermore, instead of returning to their old jobs, most of them changed their lives overnight. In the next three years, thirteen of the gang were arrested and given severe sentences in prison, totalling 307 years. Although Ronnie Biggs escaped in 1965, fleeing to Australia and then to South America, he returned to England in 2001 and was promptly arrested and returned to gaol, being released in 2009. Most of their loot was never recovered, having been spent by the thieves.

There has also been a report that the operation was supported by Otto Skorzeny, a former German paratrooper officer during the Second World War, but the truth of this intriguing tale is uncertain.

A Scottish tragedy, 1968

John Connell, aged 35, was a lorry driver, who lived with his wife and son on a house boat, named *Ace*, on the mouth of Loch Leven, near Dumbarton. A neighbour of his was Neil Gallacher, aged 27, who lived on *Viola*.

Tragedy was to occur on the Friday night of 25 February 1968. The two men were involved in a scuffle near the railway line near Balloch station, when an empty three-coach Blue train was about to pass along. Connell died of multiple injuries by being killed by the train and Gallacher was injured. He and an unnamed woman were sent to the Vale of Leven hospital that night, though she was soon released.

On 4 March, Connell was brought before the Dumbarton Sheriff's court. There was no plea or declaration for him; merely that he be remanded pending further police enquiries. He claimed he had no recollection of the fight or what happened thereafter.

The trial took place at the High Court of Glasgow on 6 May. Gallacher pleaded not guilty to the charge of having pushed Connell onto the railway line and having held him there to be killed by the train, following a fight in which the woman tried to stop them. There were no witnesses for the defence. Gallacher's plea was one of self-defence and after 20 minutes deliberation, the jury acquitted him. Afterwards, Gallacher was released and cleared up his belongings at Balloch prior to leaving the district.

Murder at night, 1985

Mrs Janet Mary Maddocks, aged 35, was in social work and worked in an office at Institute Road, King's Heath, Birmingham. She was travelling home on the night mail train on Wednesday 20 March 1985. Unfortunately, she never arrived at her destination and her corpse was later found near the railway line near Northampton.

She had been stabbed in the neck with such force that her spinal cord was severed. She had then been robbed and thrown from the train. Initially the police said they were looking for a long-haired young man who was seen leaving the train at Northampton Castle station later that night. He was described as aged about 26, was five feet six tall and might be sleeping rough. On 27 March, a reconstruction of Mrs Maddocks' last hours was undertaken.

Two days later, Jack Roy, a 15 year old from Shorebridge Road, Glasgow, was arrested in Glasgow and then charged with the murder and remanded in custody. It was not until December that he was brought to trial at Northampton Crown Court. Roy pleaded not guilty. Desmond Fennell QC said that the body may have been propped up against a window in the bloodstained carriage before being thrown out three miles later. He added that Roy found Mrs Maddocks alone in the carriage and then demanded money from her, brandishing a knife. When she refused, he killed her. According to Fennell, 'The defendant struck the knife into her throat, on the left side just near the jugular vein, with such force that it severed her spinal cord, causing almost instant paralysis.' She had then been stabbed twice in the groin, when she would have been unable to have even tried to defend herself. Death was due to shock and a massive loss of blood.

Roy had taken a late train from Milton Keynes to Glasgow when he ran into Miss Maddocks. High with the hallucinatory drug, LSD, he tried to snatch her handbag and then stabbed her to death. Justice Otton called this an 'evil and callous crime'. Roy was found guilty and sentenced on 21 January 1986.

Accident or murder? 1996

On 28 July 1996, the 26-year-old Ian Lowery was walking back to his parents' home in Churchtown, near Gloucester. He had just enjoyed his Saturday night out in the Hare and Hounds pub before going onto a social club. It was about 11.30 and he had completed about 25 minutes of his half-hour walk home. He was eager to return to watch Linford Christie at the Atlanta Olympics on TV.

What happened next is uncertain. What we know for sure is that a 85-ton maintenance train from Cheltenham to Gloucester was travelling along the railway line which bordered part of his walk home. The driver saw a body on the line near Sugar Loaf bridge. He put on the emergency brake, but it was too late. The train hit the body. Lowery's remains were found at midnight by police and his parents informed.

The police assumed that Lowery, who had been drinking, was drunk and on his way home he had toppled over a four foot high fence and then fallen forty feet down the slope near the bridge and onto the railway line the train had then crashed into him. Trains were allowed to run on the line shortly afterwards and the victim's clothes were returned to his parents.

His parents thought that their son, who was frightened of heights, would never have gone near the high bridge. They thought he had been murdered and were critical of the lack of a serious police investigation. The case was reopened in 1998 and again a few years later. However, it was probably too late. The area where the body was found was not properly searched, scuff marks on the side of the railway bridge were ignored and the victim's clothes had been returned before any forensic examination had occurred. Nor had there been a detailed examination of the corpse by a pathologist and the post mortem was minimal. Therefore, most of the forensic clues and witness evidence that might have been found by an immediate inquiry had been lost.

There were additional pointers to this being a case of murder. A man in black was seen leaning over the railway bridge on the night of the murder. His identity was never established. Lowery's money and ring were never found, pointing to this being robbery with violence. Two men were arrested, but were subsequently released due to lack of evidence. It seems probable that the young man was attacked on his way home that night for whatever cash he had with him, then pushed down onto the railway line. That said, it seems unlikely, unless further evidence comes to light, that his killer/s will ever be brought to justice.

The criminal and the student, 2008

It was once said, after nineteenth-century railway murders, that the introduction of open carriages, rather than ones divided into compartments, would prevent such crimes. Unfortunately, that was not to be and this instance is an example. Thomas Grant was a student in history and Arabic at St Andrew's University. The 19 year old was popular, had everything to live for and much to offer. Having recently completed his first year exams, he was travelling home for a holiday. He took a train from St Andrews, changing at Carlisle in order to continue his trip home. Surprisingly, like Ian Lowery, he lived in Churchtown, Gloucestershire.

Thus he was standing at a platform on Carlisle station. Hearing raised voices, he briefly turned to look at a group of three people nearby, two of whom were arguing. He then turned back to his own thoughts. The trio was made up of Thomas Lee Wood, aged 22, his girlfriend Sarah Chadwick, both from Skelmersdale, Lancashire, and who had recently been residing with Sarah Dunsheath near Carlisle. She was the third person. Wood had 21 previous convictions for 40 offences and had recently been released from a six-month sentence in gaol for burglary. He had also been known to be violent towards Miss Chadwick, whom he lived with, even though she might have been pregnant. Unbeknown to the others, he had stolen a knife from Sarah Dunsheath's kitchen and had it in his inner pocket. Wood told his girlfriend that he would steal the food she was planning to eat later that evening.

With the arrival of the southbound train, Grant, Wood and Miss Chadwick boarded the same coach. Grant sat by his bicycle and kept himself to himself. Wood and his companion continued to argue. Wood had changed the subject to railway tickets. He tore up his own and declared he would stab the ticket collector rather than be told to leave the train. His girlfriend began to cry. Then he stalked up and down the packed carriage.

During this time he saw Grant and perhaps remembered him looking at him on the platform. He took the knife and lunged down, stabbing Grant in the chest. Panic-stricken passengers, including children, fled the carriage and the train manager had the intervening door locked. They saw Wood going berserk and feared he might break through. However, he failed and, realizing the train was stopping (at Oxenholme), he escaped through a train window. Running through the fields, he took a lift from a farmer and was taken to a bus station, where he was arrested.

Wood was tried for murder at Preston Crown Court before Mr Justice Openshaw, who said, of Grant, 'He did nothing more than just look and it cost him his life'. Wood claimed that he was feeling intimidated and only meant to threaten Grant, not kill him. The motion of the train had caused him to accidentally lunge at Grant, killing him. However, he was found guilty of murder and sentenced to life imprisonment, and was told he would serve at least 21 years. It had been an unprovoked attack in a public place.

The crimes briefly noted above, do not, of course, constitute the remainder of railway murders in the United Kingdom; others include Margaret Eastwood throwing her illegitimate baby off a train near Barnes in 1938, the killing of Paul Carberry by John Murray on a train to Wembley in 1979, a stabbing on a train near New Cross in 1973 and the murder by Vaso Aliu of his former girlfriend, Marguerite van Campenhout, on a busy Underground platform in 2002.

We shall now turn, briefly, to the less unpleasant world of fictional vintage railway crime.

Sherlock Holmes and railways

Holmes and Watson would always take a train to any investigation of theirs which took place in the countryside. They travelled down to Dartmoor on a train from Paddington, for instance, in *The Hound of the Baskervilles*. Yet for travelling around London, they usually took a hansom cab. There is only one reference in the entire canon in which the Underground is taken. This may sound surprising, in light of the fact that the Baker Street tube station was very close to their lodgings at the north end of that thoroughfare. In 'The Adventure of the Red Headed League', apparently set in 1890, Holmes wished to see his client's business premises in the City. Watson states, 'We travelled by the Underground as far as Aldersgate'. Modern readers should not confuse this Metropolitan line station with Aldgate. The station is nowhere to be found on a modern Underground map. This is because it has since been renamed as the Barbican.

There is only one crime on the railway network which Holmes is called upon to investigate. This occurs in 'The Bruce Partington Plans'. It is 1895 and the corpse of one Arthur Cadogan West, a young man employed at Woolwich Arsenal, is found on the line just outside Aldgate station, which is on both the Metropolitan and Circle lines. His head 'was badly crushed'. Initially it is believed that he may have fallen or have been pushed from a train (in those days, carriage doors could be opened at any point during a journey, not just at platforms as now). Of course, he could not have been carried onto the line because the ticket collector at the gates would have seen them.

The problem is that on the young man's body are part of some top-secret submarine plans (the Bruce Partington Plans, whose 'importance can hardly be exaggerated'). However, the remainder of these plans is missing. The other problem is how could West have been found where he was? He did not have a ticket on his body. West had been in Woolwich earlier in the evening before his death. It is initially assumed that he left Woolwich and met a foreign agent in London.

Once Holmes has begun his investigation, he learns that there is no sign of any violence in any of the carriages. Nor is there any blood on the line. He deduces that West was on the roof of a carriage and was thrown onto the line when the train swayed on the railway points. Once he has access to the names and addresses of a number of spies in London, he finds that the house of one of them is adjacent to part of the Circle line near Gloucester Road tube station. It transpires that West followed a traitor, who had stolen the plans, to this house, was killed there and his body dropped onto a carriage roof as a train halted at the nearby station. The traitor and his confederate are arrested, the plans recovered and West's reputation saved.

Agatha Christie and the railways

Mention the two together and most people will think of the novel which has also been filmed, *Murder on the Orient Express*. Or perhaps *The Mystery of the Blue Train*, both of which are set on the Continent. But there are two home-grown tales, a short story featuring Hercule Poirot, 'The Plymouth Express', and a Miss Marple novel, *4.50 from Paddington* (filmed in 1962 as *Murder she Said*, starring Margaret Rutherford).

When Mrs Elspeth MacGillicuddy takes a train at 4.50 pm from Paddington, just before Christmas, the last thing she expects to witness is a murder. But that is exactly what happens when the train she is on passes another train. It is on a bend and the shutters suddenly shoot up. But all she can see is a tall, broad man strangling a woman and cannot see his face. When she reports this to the railway staff and the police, they are polite and go through the motions. This is because the police cannot find a corpse. Without a corpse, there can be no murder inquiry.

Undeterred, she turns to her old friend, Miss Marple. She sets about trying to solve the mystery. With help from a young nephew who is an employee of British Railways, she concludes that the train that was passed was the 4.33 stopping service from Paddington. The trains would have passed near to the edge of the rambling country estate which surrounds Rutherford Hall. As she astutely observes, a murder on a train gives the killer the advantage of anonymity. She realizes that, if a killing occurs where someone lives, the killer might be seen coming or going, and if he drives his victim to a location, however, remote, someone may see him or notice the car. But on a train, with many passengers coming and going, all the killer needs to do is to leave at the next station, and if it is a busy one, he is unlikely to be remembered.

Miss Marple then calls on the services of the astute young Lucy Eylesbarrow, who agrees to take a temporary post at the house whilst searching for clues. She finds traces of clothing near the brambles close to the railway line. She later discovers the body of a strangled woman in the Old Barn on the estate. Much of the book then concerns the identity of the victim. Could it be something to do with the Crackenthorpe family, most of whom do not live there, but are regular visitors?

The killer turns out to be someone totally unexpected. He had been living apart from his wife. Then he sees the opportunity to marry a rich woman. So he contacts his wife and suggests a reconciliation and they meet in London and travel from Paddington. There he kills her, without having been witnessed, or so he thinks, and then throws the body out near Rutherford Hall. That evening he takes the body and hides it in the Old Barn. In the forthcoming weeks, he proceeds to murder other members of the family, so his hoped for future bride will be all the more wealthy. An excellent plan – but foiled by Miss Marple and her allies.

Conclusion

Sherlock Holmes observed in *A Study in Scarlet* that 'There is nothing new under the sun. It has all been done before.' Whether it was Thomas Briggs being killed by Francis Muller in 1864 or Patricia Woolard falling victim to Michael Gills just over a century later, the pattern of the railway murder is depressingly the same. In almost all instances, the killer and his victim meet together in a railway compartment. The killer almost always is armed and takes his victim, usually a weaker individual as well, by total surprise. The motive is usually robbery, though not always. The weapon used is often a gun, but can also be a knife or a bludgeon. The victim has little chance. Then the killer either makes his escape or is caught.

Of the twenty-five victims in this book, ten were men, eleven were women and there were four children. Four were shot, nine were stabbed or slashed, two were strangled, four were bludgeoned and six killed by trains. Twenty-one were killed by strangers and four by those known to them. Money was the motivation behind eight murders, sex/love by four and in eight murders the motive is unknown. Two resulted from arguments, one was due to insanity and two were accidental. Of these killers, fifteen were apprehended and ten escaped unscathed. This is a high proportion of unsolved crimes, because in the 1920s/1930s, the clear-up rate of murders in London was over 90 per cent. The reason for this is that most of these murders were crimes committed by strangers and these are the most difficult to solve, because there is no prior connection between killer and victim. Trains can be transitory and anonymous places, where people only spend a fleeting time and then depart. Almost all the killers, without question, were male – murder being predominantly a man's crime. The exception, perhaps, is the killing of Willie Starchfield in 1914, where a woman might have been responsible.

Compared to those crimes committed in detective novels, railway murders are not carefully thought out ones, requiring a master sleuth to unravel them. Serious thefts from trains, whether in 1855 or in 1963, did require much planning and nerve on the part of the thieves. Both succeeded in taking the money and escaping unscathed. However, in both cases, the criminals ended up being arrested and gaoled through their own idiocies thereafter.

Is there any consolation for passengers on trains seeking to avoid the fates of Florence Shore, Beatrice Meadmore, Frederick Gold and the others whose deaths have been related here? First, travelling alone can be dangerous. Choosing a compartment to travel in which there are other people, preferably similar to the passenger, is advice given by police. The introduction of greater surveillance techniques, such as CCTV cameras may also assist in detecting crime after it has happened, though railway crimes still occur in the twenty-first century, as we have noted. One only has to think of the woman attacked and nearly killed for remonstrating with youths at a suburban station in London, or a gang of youths who attacked and robbed passengers on the Underground. But, as said, the percentage of crimes committed on board trains is very small, and the main risk to life and limb when railbound, and it is statistically a tiny one, is to be involved in a train crash. Bon voyage!

Bibliography

PRIMARY SOURCES
The National Archives
ADM159/29, 35, ASSI36/139 (Dean), ASSI36/522 (Woolard),
CRIM1/1080 (Waters), DPP/2/4222 (Woolard), MEPO3/75-76
(Briggs), MEPO3/169 (Money), MEPO3/1627 (Mays), PCOM8/409
(Mays), RAIL635/196.
The Wellcome Institute Library
PP/SP1/2, 5 (Spilsbury autopsy index cards)
Newspapers
Aldershot News, 1952, 1965
Annual Register, 1864, 1884
Brighton and Hove Advertiser, 1914
Brighton Times, 1914
Croydon Advertiser, 1875, 1945
Croydon Chronicle, 1875
Croydon Times, 1945
Cumberland Herald, 1962
Hackney Gazette, 1927
Hants and Berks Gazette, 1964
Hastings and St Leonards Observer, 1920
Illustrated Police News, 1901, 1910
Middlesex County Times, 1920
Newcastle Daily Chronicle, 1910
St Leonard's Chronicle, 1920
Sussex Express, 1920
The Times, 1855, 1864, 1875, 1881, 1901, 1910, 1915, 1927, 1985
Wembley News, 1942
Other primary sources
E Nicholls, *Crime within the Square Mile* (1935)
*Darling Child: The Private Correspondence of Queen Victoria and the Crown
  Princess of Prussia, 1871–1878*, ed. R Fulford (1976)

The Letters of Charles Dickens, ed. G Storey, vol. 10 (1998)

SECONDARY SOURCES

R Erickson, *Dictionary of Western Australia (Bond), 1829–1914*, vol. 2 (1979)

S Fielding, *The Hangman's Record*, vol. 1, *1868–1899* (1994), vol. 2, *1900–1928* (1995)

J Goodman, *The Railway Murders* (1984)

J D Oates, *Unsolved Murders in Victorian and Edwardian London* (2007)

— *Unsolved London Murders: The 1920s and 1930s* (2009)

— *Unsolved London Murders: 1940s and 1950s* (2009)

Oxford Dictionary of National Biography, vol. 3 (2004)

J Whitbread, *The Railway Policeman* (1961)

Index